THE DIARY OF A COTSWOLD FOXHUNTING LADY 1905-1910

FRANCES WITTS

Illustrated by Susan Boone
Edited jointly by Lavina Jenkinson and Susan Boone

AMBERLEY

The editor and illustrator thanked the following for their assistance with this enterprise:-

Ronald Boone
Susan Scaramanga
Olive Baker
Violet Barlow
Leslie Brain

This book was originally dedicated to
John: Brother and Friend

First published 2008

Amberley Publishing
The Hill, Merrywalks
Stroud, Gloucestershire, GL5 4EP
www.amberley-books.com

The photographs and paintings in this book reproduced
by courtesy of Michael Boone and Francis E. B. Witts

British Library Cataloguing in Publication Data.
A catalogue record for this book is available from the British Library.

ISBN *978-1-84868-020-3*

Typesetting and origination by Amberley Publishing
Printed and bound in Great Britain

FOREWORD

Susan Boone was the eldest daughter of Jack and Frances Kennard. She was brought up in Scotland, but spent her holidays at Guiting Grange and at Eyford Park. Her passions were horses, painting and her children. She learnt to paint at the Byam Shaw School in London and married Ronald Boone during the Second World War. Susan illustrated this book in 1981, after which, a small private edition was produced jointly with Lavinia Jenkinson. Susan and Lavinia both died shortly afterwards. This is the first commercial publication.

This edition contains a colour section featuring many paintings by Susan Boone. The other photographs in the book are mainly from the family collection held by Michael Boone.

PREFACE

by Captain R.E Wallace, M.F.H
to the original private edition published in 1981

This is the diary of Frances Witts, written between 1905 and 1910. It will be read with great interest by those who enjoy hunting with the Heythrop and the North Cotswold. They describe the sport when Charles Sturman, one of the great hound breeders and then at the height of his skill, was hunting the Heythrop country; and when Mr Brassey was still reigning with supreme power. They also mention many days with the North Cotswold and Cotswold hounds, with their comparisons in style. It is fascinating to find that foxes ran much the same sort of lines as they appear to do today, with ambitious points in all the Gloucestershire hills. When the hounds ventured as far as Adderbury the ease with which foxes were caught must have been more satisfactory for the huntsman than the followers, until the afternoon sport when progress was made back towards Chipping Norton. The big difference seems to have been the distance between coverts drawn, and the necessity to hack back into the original draw after a long morning hunt in those days.

The diaries also touch upon the logisitics of life of seventy years ago, and have been compiled by two people well qualified to do so. Susan Boone is related to those who owned and cared for much of the Cotswold hills, and has been devoted to that part of the world and the hunting of it all her life. Lavinia Jenkinson's contribution to the maintenance of country affairs throughout the Heythrop terrain is a legend in itself.

I hope that many sportsmen will read and enjoy the diaries.

INTRODUCTION

by Susan Boone

I am introducing this diary with a short history of the main characters in the Waddingham/Witts and Brassey families.

MOTHER

'Mother' of the diaries was Margaret Waddingham, my grandmother. She was born in Leeds in 1843. At the age of three she and her two elder brothers were brought by her father, John Waddingham, to Guiting Grange. He had bought the house — a pleasant Georgian one — altered it to the Italian style fashionable at that time, and built on a servants' wing. He doubled the size of the park and built a great wall round it. The estate consisted of the Home Farm, Naunton Inn Farm, Round Hill, Aylworth and Naunton Downs Farms.

Mother married Frederick Witts in 1876. He was the second son of the Rector and Lord of the Manor of Upper Slaughter. He, the Rector, must have ruled the people of the village body and soul. Frederick's relation, Vavasour of Stow, gave them Fosse Cottage (now Fosseway House) outside Stow in the parish of Broadwell, as a wedding present. She rebuilt it into a large house where her three daughters were born.

When the diaries begin Sophia was aged 28, Mabel 27 and Frances 24.

Frances Witts and Jack Kennard, 9 August 1910.

HMS *Repulse*, the battlecruiser on which Jack Kennard served during the First World War.

Jack Kennard.

In 1908, her brother John having died childless and her brother James having no children, she inherited Guiting Grange. Frederick died in 1900, aged 57. She moved to Guiting Grange and made many improvements to the garden and estate. In 1910 she married Mabel and Frances in great style. She died in 1918 not having allowed her daughters to see her in her last illness.

She was, in a way, a typical Victorian lady, strict and traditional. In other ways she was adventurous and forward-looking, belonging to the 20th century. She herself taught her children to ride and took them out hunting, never sending them with a groom. She encouraged her eldest daughter, Sophie, to be a doctor. The farm cottages she built on the estate had a tap in the house as well as other modern improvements. She planted a fox cover — Mrs. Waddingham's Gorse.

Her great-grandchildren and her great-great-grand-children are still hunting with the Heythrop.

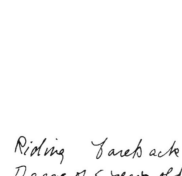

Riding bareback using halters.
After the age of 5 years old the girls were not allowed to ride astride

EYFORD KNOLL

SOPHIA

She was the brains of the family. In her early 20's she fell in love and wished to marry her Uncle James's agent. (Uncle James had an estate in Wales). This match was not thought good enough and was quashed by Mother. Sophie fell back on her other love — medicine; this was encouraged by Mother. Having been educated by governesses she had no biology, physics or mathematics necessary for the first MB, so she lodged in London and studied at a London University College. She was accepted as a medical student at the Royal Free Hospital, Grays Inn Road (the only London hospital to take women) and she qualified. This is the reason she is only mentioned hunting in the diaries during holiday time.

Litter of Foxcubs in hollow tree at end of drive

In World War I she was practising in Sheffield. There she met Samuel Richardson, a master cutler older than herself whom she married. After the war they both retired from their professions and settled at Guiting Grange, which had been left to her. They lived there very happily till he died. As children we frequently stayed there and loved our Uncle Sam. I think his death must have broken her heart; it certainly changed her; she became frail. The estate became too much for her and she sold Round Hill, Aylworth and Naunton Downs farms. In 1936 she decided to move to warmer climes — Prestbury and then Penzance. She had become very religious and high church — to Mabel's and Frances's disgust, the family being strongly mid-Anglican. She gave Guiting Grange to Francie, Mabel being already doyen of Eyford Park. She died after Francie and left half the family money to the church, which was very detrimental to the future of Guiting Grange. It was a pity that someone so intelligent, kind and elegant as I remember her should become such a sad person.

Margaret Waddingham's great grandchildren & great great grandchildren still hunt with the Heythrop.

David Van Royen "Candid" Charlotte van Roven "Bracken" Joanna Van Royen "Coreander"

MABEL

The beauty of the family. She had fair hair and brown eyes. In 1910 she married Jack Cheetham and lived the rest of her life at Eyford Park. They bred, broke and schooled on hunters and lived a happy, country life. She gave refuge to Francie and her family when she was between sea ports, and kept a pony for her nephews and nieces. She lent me Eyford Knoll, which was built by Sir Guy Dauber, and was the farm house for Eyford Home Farm. It was vacant as the farm was being worked by Don Hanks at Summerhill. After she died she left it to me. Ronnie Wallace bought it and lived there after we moved to Rockcliffe, Dower house of Eyford. She died at Eyford in 1961 having hunted for nearly 70 seasons with the Heythrop.

FRANCIE — MY MOTHER

She was fair haired, grey eyed, and great fun. Born at Fosse Cottage, in 1881; she was sent to Winchester High School when she was 17 for one year, which she much enjoyed and made many friends including Dolly Jervoise Smith of Sandwell, Totnes, with whom she stayed to hunt with the Dartmoor

On the Heythrop hunting field she met Jack Kennard a Naval Officer, who sometimes spent a leave with his grandfather, Mr Byass of Wyck Hill, a retired merchant banker. Her tall hat fell off. He galloped to pick it up. His horse put its foot through it. He was always rather a sailor on horseback. It must have been a nerve-racking business courting under Mother's eagle eye (although the hunting field has always been a good place in which to court). Jack quailed when it came to asking Mother for Frances's hand, the Kennard family fortune having taken one of its perennial downward plunges. He wisely took his own Mother along with him and the day was won. They were married in August 1910, four weeks after Mabel.

Francie & Co. arriving at station to stay at Eyford

After the honeymoon Frances 'followed the flag' from seaport to seaport — 12 houses in 10 years. She had four children who trailed after her. In 1922 Jack left the Navy, having inherited the job of Director of Falkirk Iron Foundry. This he ran like a ship and successfully. The 1929 crisis forced an amalgamation; the family foundry became part of the Allied Iron Foundries. Francie lived in a works house — a nice house and garden with stables, but surrounded on two sides by the foundry, on one side the railway and on the third a slum tenement. However, the foundry used horses for transport so there was a field for Frances's hunter and her children's ponies. We went out hunting with the Linlithgow & Stirlingshire, riding to the meet through the town. The nearest meet was three miles away so we had mammoth rides and sometimes we went by train. Francie, in the most unlikely area, somehow created a little Guiting Grange. She was given Guiting Grange in 1936 when Jack would have retired and they would have gone to live at Guiting Grange. However, the war came, he was still on the Royal Naval Reserve and could have commanded a convoy. However, his orders were to stay in his job and make weapons. After the war both were over 60.

They lived at Guiting Grange, which had been occupied by the Army and was therefore rather battered. To start with they lived by lamplight, rather cold until Jack installed wood-burning forrester stoves which he had invented. Francie died in 1949 aged 68 so did not long enjoy living at Guiting Grange, which was my family's dream place to live. Jack lived on there until he died in 1967. Frances's eldest son, Bobby, inherited but it was financially and practically impossible to live in such a house — huge rooms needing cheap coal to warm them and legions of servants to run it. He sold it to a millionaire, but even he could not cope with the house. He pulled it down and converted part of the stables into a dwelling house. Nowadays the fox runs across the site of Guiting Grange.

Like his father before him doctors & hunts
in the Heythrop country

THE BRASSEYS

Of the Brassey's I do not know so much, although quite a lot from what I have heard. They were all descendants of a very remarkable man one of a quartet who built the railways of North America and elsewhere in the world, each making an enormous fortune. He was Thomas Brassey.

Albert, second son, bought Heythrop, formerly a hunting box which the Duke of Beaufort used when he came to what was then the north side of the Beaufort country. It had been partially destroyed by fire so Albert re-built it. His son, Bobby, built Brassey Buildings and a farmhouse for the land of Upper Slaughter. Albert lived in wonderful style at Heythrop, where the hounds were kennelled, and was Master for 36 years. He was much loved and respected in the country. He had eight children; they all hunted and were mostly a few years older than my Mother. At the time of the diaries most of them were married and having babies. Mother obviously admired them very much. When they 'were not out' obviously they were having a baby.

Mr. Albert Brassey

Rosie, the second daughter, who married Captain Daly, was my Godmother. He came from Ireland.

Henry, the third son, built Copse Hill as a hunting box and hired a special train to bring his family, their horses, dogs, pets, servants, carriages, luggage and children from Kent to Bourton-on-the-Water. Its arrival was greeted by the people lining the bridge halloa-ing. His son, Harold, eventually lived at Copse Hill. He had the house altered by Lutyens, who also built cottages round Bagehot Square, near to the churchyard in Upper Slaughter. He sold it to Bobby in order to move to Leicestershire for better hunting than he thought the Heythrop could provide. Henry's youngest son, Edwin, left the Army and bought Copse Hill from Bobby and lived there till he died. Edwin was joint Master of the Heythrop for many years.

Albert's and Henry's great-grandchildren and great-great-grandchildren still hunt with the Heythrop.

Henry's great-grandson, Robert Cookson, became joint Master of the Heythrop in 1979.

BRASSEY FAMILY TREE

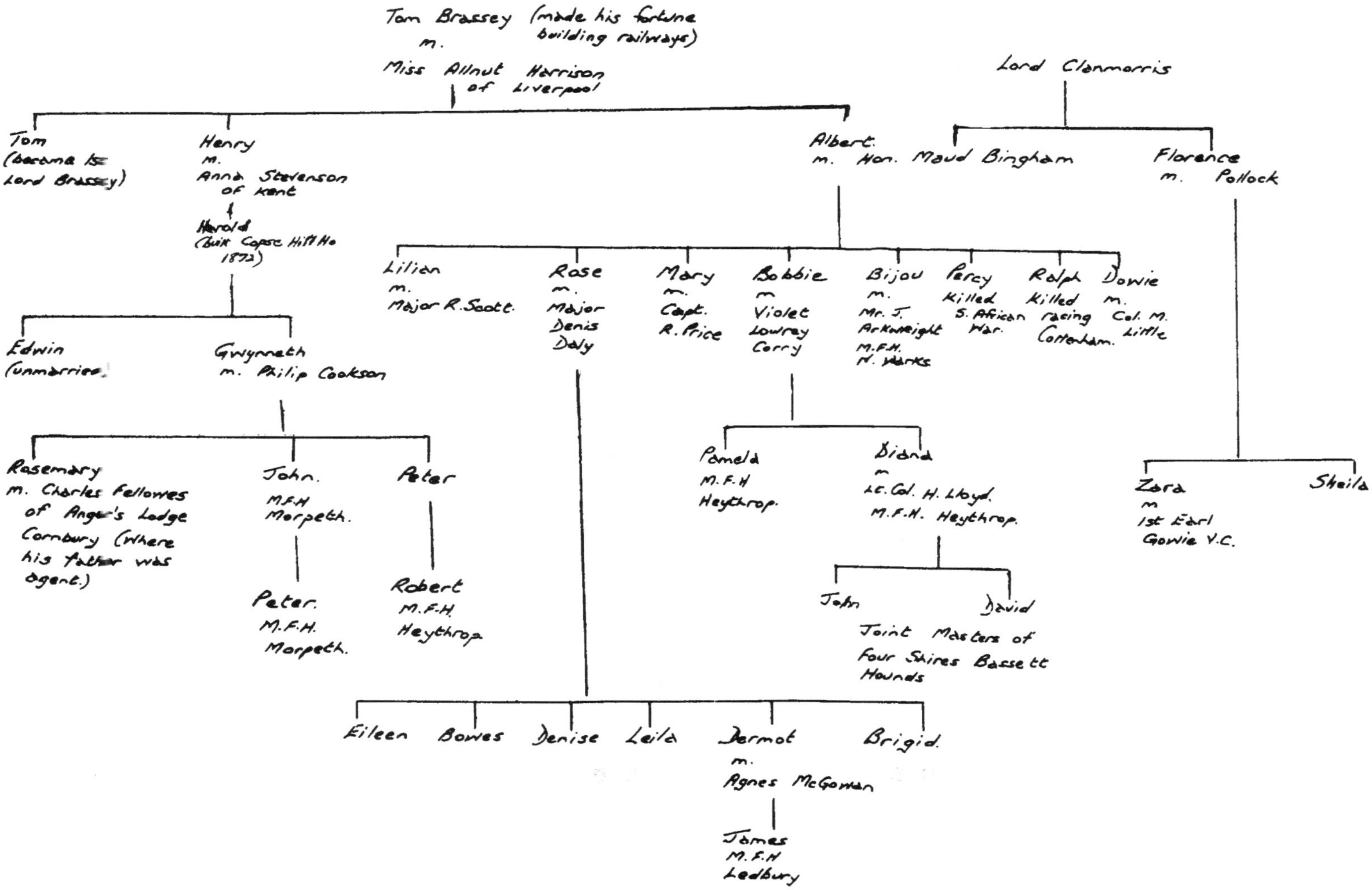
Tom Brassey (made his fortune building railways)
m.
Miss Allnut Harrison of Liverpool
Lord Clanmorris
Tom (became 1st Lord Brassey)
Henry
m.
Anna Stevenson of Kent
Harold (Built Copse Hill Ho 1872)
Albert.
m. Hon. Maud Bingham
Florence
m. Pollock
Edwin (unmarried
Gwynneth
m. Philip Cookson
Lilian
m.
Major R. Scott.
Rose
m.
Major Denis Daly
Mary
m.
Capt. R. Price
Bobbie
m
Violet Lowrey Corry
Bijou
m.
Mr. J. Arkwright M.F.H. N. Warks
Percy
Killed S. African War.
Ralph
Killed racing Cottenham.
Dowie
m.
Col. M. Little
Rosemary
m. Charles Fellowes of Anger's Lodge Cornbury (where his father was agent.)
John.
M.F.H
Morpeth.
Peter
Peter.
M.F.H.
Morpeth.
Robert
M.F.H.
Heythrop
Pamela
M.F.H
Heythrop.
Diana
m
Lt. Col. H. Lloyd.
M.F.H. Heythrop.
John
David
Joint Masters of Four Shires Bassett Hounds
Zara
m
1st Earl Gowrie V.C.
Sheila
Eileen
Bowes
Denise
Leila
Dermot
m.
Agnes McGowan
Brigid.
James
M.F.H
Ledbury

BOURTON-ON-THE-WATER
Henry Brassey Family arrive from Kent on special Trai

Masters of the packs mentioned in the diaries during this period were as follows:—

Heythrop — Mr Albert Brassey
Cotswold — Mr H. O. Lord
North Cotswold — Sir John Hume-Campbell, 1906-1908
Sir John Hume-Campbell and Captain C. T. Scott, 1908-1910
North Warwickshire — Mr J. P. Arkwright, 1901-1906
Mr J. P. Arkwright and Lord Algernon Percy, 1906-1907
Mr J. P. Arkwright, 1907-1908
Hon. Alexander Parker, 1908-1912

Albert Brassey's great great grandchildren still hunt with The Heythrop

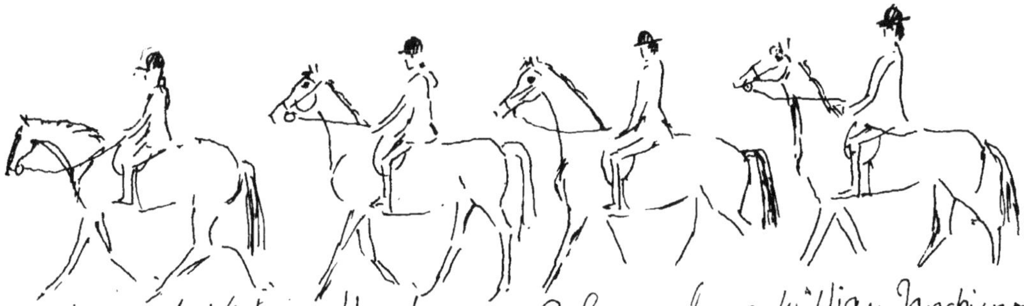

eorgina and Victoria Lloyd   Alexander & William Mackinnon

I have drawn quite a few scenes from Agriculture. Foxhunting could not continue to exist without the goodwill, indeed the permission, of the farmers.

Many of them hunt either on horses, or these days, follow in the car. So I hope they are rewarded in pleasure for their generosity.

The farmworkers are equally tolerant and useful, telling the huntsmen where the fox has gone. Several have told me that they like their 'bit of hunting'.

Lucinda and

Arabella Cecil

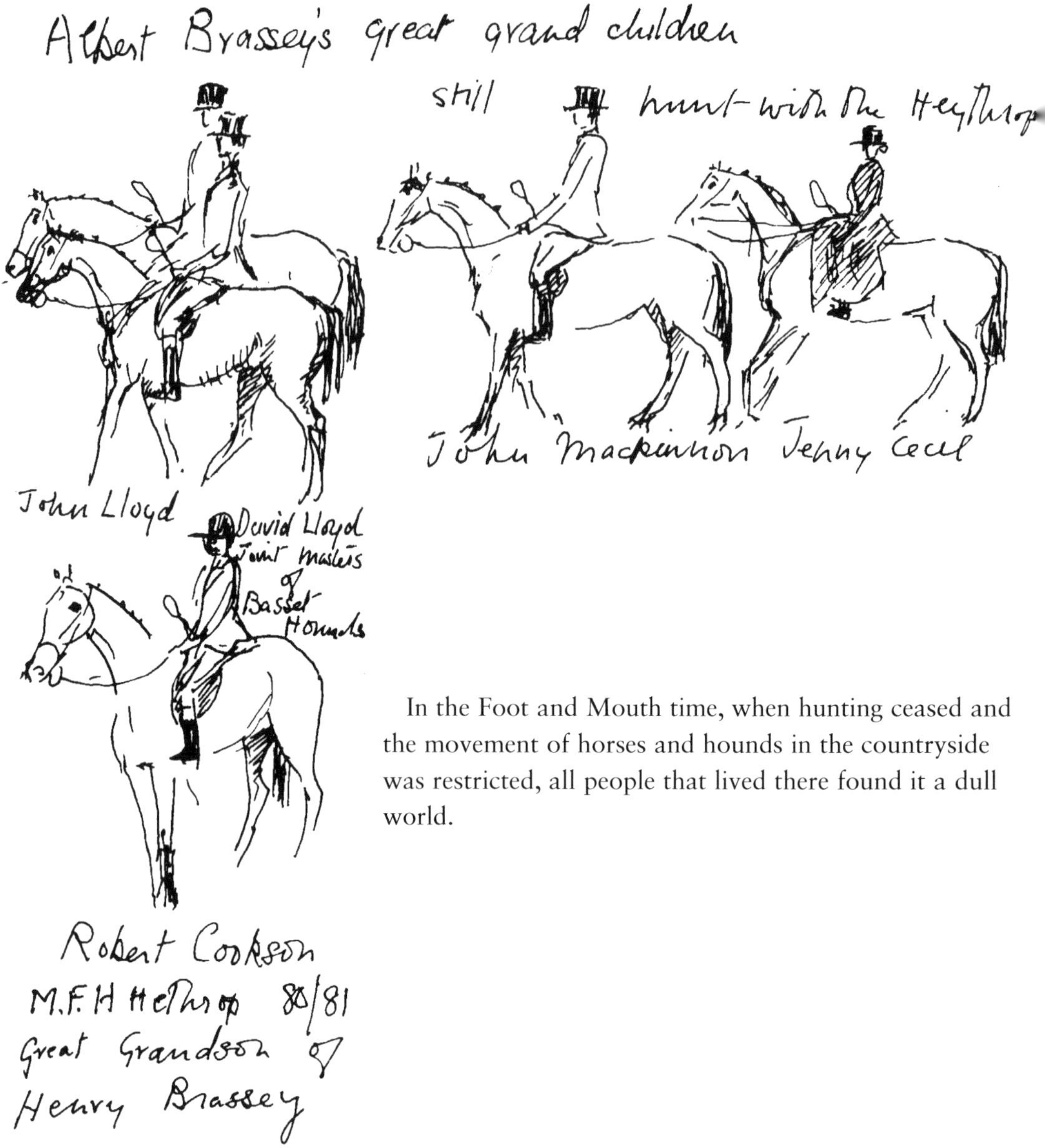

In the Foot and Mouth time, when hunting ceased and the movement of horses and hounds in the countryside was restricted, all people that lived there found it a dull world.

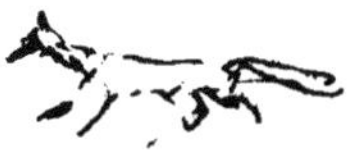

SEASON 1905 - 1906

Monday, Sept. 4th

Adlestrop.
First day's cubbing at 5 o'clock on N. Pritchard's Chestnut mare. *(Norah Pritchard of Donnington later married Mr Lee of Broadwell Manor).*

Drew Adlestrop Hill and Harcomb.

"Here comes Brassey: dogs Foxhounds and all!"

Friday, Sept. 29th

Bourton Wood. Cubbing on Mr Fenwick's grey. *(The creator of the famous Abbotswood Gardens).*

Monday, Oct. 30th

Heythrop. Rode De Wet, Mabel rode Rex.

Mabel and I stayed at Over Norton. Bad day.

Said Thomas Harris carter to Thomas Gayden Farmer of Lower Swell

Friday, Nov. 3rd

New Barn. Rode Shamrock, Mabel rode King John.

Horses not in condition. Good run over the walls. Shamrock lame next day.

Monday, Nov. 6th

Kineton Thorns. Rode Judith, Mabel rode Kate. N. Cotswold.

Horses not in condition. Not a good day. Judith very fresh and went well but sometimes stumbled landing. Not to hunt her again because not safe—very sad.

Mabel Witts and Jack Cheetham, 7 July 1910.

Centre and right, Revd. Canon Broome Witts and his brother George Witts.

warrior "looked at"

Monday, Nov. 13th

Pomfret Castle. Rode Shamrock, Mabel rode Johnnie.

Bad day. Mr Brain of Brailes offered us horse he was riding. Rather common looking.

Wednesday, Nov. 15th

Chipping Norton Junc. *(Kingham Station)*. Rode Pearman's mare Eva, Mabel rode Kate.

Found Bould Wood. Killed between Idbury and Fifield. Went straight on after another fox which, after a hunting run, was killed in cover above Milton. Frightfully cold day. Liked Eva fairly well.

warrior "tried"

Friday, Nov. 17th

Bourton-on-the-Water. Rode Shamrock, Mabel rode Johnnie.

Ground very hard and slippery after two nights' frost. Terrified of slippery banks by Redesdale's gorse. Found Redesdale's Gorse. Ran by Naunton to Eyford where lost. Fox got up in field and ran for about 5 minutes; to ground in drainpipe.

Mabel, J. Godman *(of Banks Fee)* and I spent long time refusing small fence.

Found in cover near Aston Grove and ran slowly near Farmington Grove and lost near Gilbert's grave—out by ourselves for first time.

warrior "tried"

Monday, Nov. 20th

Chapel House. Rode Mr Brain's horse to see whether would buy. Mr Brain rode Shamrock.

Found at Walk Gorse, ran fast to Rollright where lost. Found Walk Gorse ran by Over Norton and lost near Chapel House. Chopped fox in Walk Gorse. Found Salford Osiers, ran fast for a few fields and lost near Kennels. Liked horse very much. Wish he were a bit faster, but a splendid fencer.

warrior Bought

Friday, Nov. 24th

Moreton. Rode Mr Brain's horse Warrior, which Mother has bought for £80. Mabel rode Kate.

Found Blackthorns, very fast circling run and lost near Bourton Wood. Was left behind; only about twelve people got it, Mother and Mabel amongst them. Got on Shamrock and spent a long time in Bourton Wood and Batsford. Found below Cadley Arbour and ran by Aston Magna, where we rather mixed with the North Cotswold; on close to Moreton, through Sezincote and gave up near Cadley Arbour. Some of N. Cotswold hounds joined ours and had to be separated in stable yard at Batsford. I rather lost myself with the N. Cotswold at Aston Magna. Shamrock jumped a gate very nicely.

Wednesday, Nov. 29th

Oddington. Rode Shamrock, Mabel rode King John.

Found at Oddingon Ashes and killed within two fields of Stow Bridge Copse. Mother, Mabel and I all left behind in Ashes. not many people with the hounds.

Found Gawcomb, ran up the vale nearly to Bould Wood, then turned onto the hill, and dragged on to Tangley, where a fox was killed. Got the run very well. Shamrock jumped very fairly. Found Icomb Cow Pastures, ran by Botany Bay and towards Gawcomb.

Friday, Dec. 1st

Evenlode. Rode Warrior, Mabel Kate, Mother Spider & Marmion.

Found in small cover near Moreton brook, ran in circle through Evenlode Mains and to ground between there and Moreton. Quite pleasant. Found Harcombs and ran very well to Evenlode Mains, then dragged down to railway line and back to Harcombs. I got away very well and Warrior went splendidly. Mr Evered very nearly jumped on Rosie Daly (see Brassey Tree) but did not do more than kick her hat. It looked as if she would be killed. Later on in day, after I had gone home, Mr Fenwick (of Abbotswood) had his horse staked and it had to be shot. A great many falls. Ground very wet.

Rosie Daly's hat kicked

Wednesday, Dec. 6th

Buckland Cross Roads. North Cotswold.
Rode Warrior, Mabel King John, Mother Marmion.

Quite a nice gallop in the vale and lost.

Friday, Dec. 8th

Farmington Grove. Rode Warrior, Mabel King John & Kate, Mother Spider.

Very small field and no pink coats. Found at Farmington Grove and ran towards Sherborne but had to be whipped off because shooting. Drew all about Turkdean and Aston Grove and Redesdale's Gorse but did not find. Suppose foxes had been stopped in. Found, after I went home, in Clapton Gorse and killed at once. Spider jumped a gate by mistake and came down. Neither the worse.

Monday, Dec. 11th

Pomfret Castle. Rode Rosie Daly's Rex, Mabel King John, Mother Marmion.

Frost in ground, so very bad going. Found Badger's Gorse, dragged on through Over Norton and lost.

Brassey sons-in-law going to the meet

Found in The Ovens, Heythrop, ran near the house, left-handed to Walk Gorse, took on presumably fresh fox and ran fast to Swerford and back to Walk Gorse and killed in the open between Walk Gorse and Heythrop. Very good hunting run of about 2 hrs. Rex a ripping mount. Was kicked twice which gave me fits. Saw Ralph's grave on the way home. Never saw such masses of lovely flowers. Poor Brasseys. *(This was Albert Brassey's son, who was killed racing at Cottenham, near Cambridge).*

Wednesday, Dec. 13th

Adlestrop. Rode Warrior, Mabel Kate, Mother Spider.

Found Oddington Ashes but could not do much. Found Icomb Cow Pastures and ran below Icomb, across Gawcomb ditch, below Idbury, turned left-handed over Gawcomb ditch close to Bledington. Warrior jumped it beautifully. Checked; on again by the Stow junction line, turned left-handed, through Icomb Cow Pastures, across Gawcomb Vale and lost near Idbury. Well up all the time thanks to Warrior. Found Gawcomb and ran along side of hill through Little Rissington and lost near Tangley. Mabel very sad as Kate got puffed and could not keep up.

Hounds whipped off on account of shooting

Friday, Dec. 15th

Moreton. Rode Shamrock, Mother Marmion.

Bad day. Drew Crawthornes, Donnington, Banks Fee, Dibden's Gorse. Plenty of foxes but could do nothing. Shamrock contrary and refusing.

Monday, Dec. 18th

Chapel House. I rode Shamrock & Warrior, Mabel King John & Kate, Mother Marmion.

Found at Walk Gorse, ran small circle and lost. Found Salford Osiers and ran towards Walk Gorse, turned left-handed in small cover on side of hill in Warwickshire country opposite Wychford Wood.

Drew Harcombs blank!

Found below Adlestrop Hill, ran through Harcombs and across vale to below Cross Hands, up and over past Roman Camp, past Adlestrop village, past Harcombs, and hounds got away in dark and fog in direction of Barton Grove, with no one with them. Shamrock went much better, and Warrior went beautifully in afternoon run.

Warrior jumping Gawcombe Ditch

Friday, Dec. 22nd

New Barn. Rode Shamrock, Mabel King John, Mother Spider.

Found Lodge Park. Ran out the other side, turned left-handed and along parallel to New Barn, Barrington New Inn road, skirted Barrington village, passed Dodd's Mill, through Sherborne Cow Pastures, below Clapton village, turned right-handed across Bourton Vale, through Rissington Common, passed Tangley on our right, close to Idbury, and killed in Bould Wood. About 2 hrs. and 20 minutes. First part as far as Barrington very nice; after that slow and over bad country. Shamrock rather contrary. Hounds did not draw again.

Shamrock contrary and refusing

Thursday, Dec. 28th

Burford. Rode Warrior, Mabel King John, Mother Spider.

Did not find till about 1.30 in gorse near Bradwell Grove, nice little gallop and lost.

Found Bradwell Grove, ran very fast and to ground in drain, about 30 minutes; very nice.

Dreadful crowd of V.W.H. and Old Berkshire out. Warrior pulling and rather mad, rushing his walls and nearly jumping me off. Rosie Daly out again and Mrs Scott, and Mrs Bobby Brassey. *(Lilian Brassey, from Williamstrip Park).*

Shamrock contrary

Saturday, Dec. 30th

Merrymouth. I rode Shamrock, Mabel Kate.

Very foggy, so went round by Taynton to Barrington. Found there and ran a few fields towards Tangley and lost. Found in Tangley, ran two fields and lost. Drew Rissington Common etc. blank and went home. Hopeless day.

Monday, Jan. 1st

Stretton-on-Fosse. (Warwickshire Hounds). Rode Warrior, Mrs Godman chaperoned me.

Drew neutral country blank. Found Golden Cross, dragged on for a bit and lost. Seemed to be foot people all over the place purposely to head fox. They did not find again while we were out. Came home from about 2 miles other side of Shipston-on-Stour. Warrior pulling rather. Rotten day.

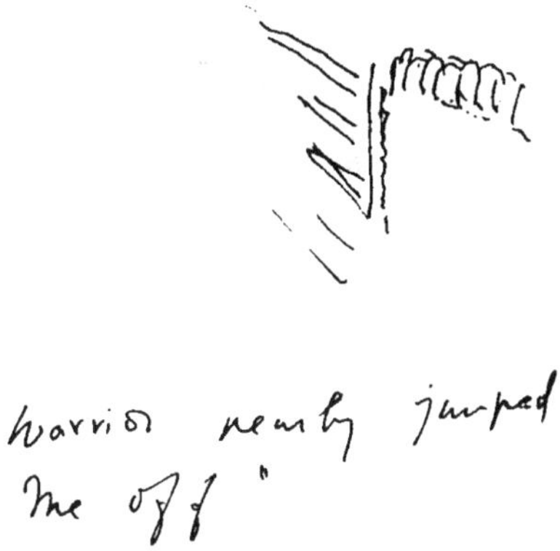
Warrior nearly jumped me off"

Wednesday, Jan. 3rd.

Springhill Lodges. N. Cotswold. Rode Shamrock, Mabel Kate, Mother at home with cold.

Thick fog on hills so went down into the vale. Fox jumped up just outside Gallipot, ran very fast over point-to-point race course, past Childswickham, turned left-handed just short of Leaslow Brakes and to ground in Buckland Wood. Very nice gallop but I lost them in Leaslow Brakes where they turned short back. Fog having cleared they drew Springhill and found. They ran past Broadway Tower, over Broadway golf links and lost by Norton House.

Warrior pulling

Friday, Jan. 5th

Stow-on-the-Wold. Rode Warrior, Mabel King John, Mother Marmion & Spider.

Found Slaughter Copses and ran through Stow Bridge Copse and lost somewhere between Bourton and Little Rissington. Had to cross brook twice — very nearly bogged both times. Found Stow Bridge Copse, ran to Slaughter Copse, right-handed past Hyde Mill, through Wyck Hill and into Gawcomb and lost. Returned to Stow Bridge Copse and did not find. Drew Copse Hill blank. Found in Slaughter New Plantations and ran through Copse Hill and to ground in drain by Slaughter Gas House.

Found in Abbotswood Cover and ran past Swell Osiers, left Banks Fee on left, through Donnington and lost near Moreton Road cutting. Not a good day. Country most frightfully deep.

Monday, Jan. 8th

Pomfret Castle. Rode Shamrock, Mabel King John, Mother Marmion.

Found Badger's Gorse and ran out towards Rollright and lost. Found in The Ovens, Heythrop, ran very fast for about 5 minutes and to ground. Found in a Heythrop cover and ran out by Enstone but turned back to Heythrop and lost. Did not find again. Mr Brassey came out in the afternoon for the first time. Rotten day : going bad.

Wednesday, Jan. 10th

Gawcomb. Rode Warrior. Mabel tried new horse, then Kate. Mother Spider.

Found Gawcomb and ran out towards Rissington and lost. Fox jumped up in gateway near Stow Bridge Copse, ran up through Wyck Hill and killed in bottom of Gawcomb. Fox holloaed out top end of Gawcomb but soon lost. Drew Botany Bay blank. Found Maugersbury Grove ran to Icomb but soon lost. Found Icomb Cow Pastures, ran out as far as line between Stow and junction, turned left-handed through Oddington, Lower Ashes, Maugersbury Grove and left-handed over hill to Icomb and lost.

Mabel did not think horse worth buying. She then got on Kate who was going so feeling that she went home. Going very bad indeed.

Heading the fox

Friday, Jan. 12th

Farmington Grove. Rode Shamrock, Mabel King John, Marmion ill so Mother had nothing to ride.

Farmington Grove blank. Found Sherborne Cow Pastures, crossed water meadows and river to Barrington and Sherborne road running well but then could do no more. Fox holloaed away from top of Cow Pastures but soon lost.

Messed round drawing little covers but at last found in cover the other side Sherborne House; ran through Farmington Grove to Sherborne Cow Pastures and soon lost. Messed round, drawing more little covers but did not find again. Capt. Daly let a little of his temper go at Mr Crowder and told him either to go home or hold his tongue! — which was the only excitement in a hopelessly bad day.

Nearly bogged in Brook

Monday, Jan. 15th

Chapel House. Rode Warrior, then Shamrock.

Found at once at Walk Gorse, ran across line and on very well up wind for about 10 minutes, then hounds divided and did not run really well again though we dragged on for some time. Found again at Walk Gorse, out towards Heythrop, back again through Walk Gorse, across line and lost near Great Rollright. Drew Salford Osiers blank. But was consoled by mince-pie brought me hot by Mrs Daly!! Found in young laurel cover on Adlestrop Hill, ran down across hill, turned back over hill to Chastleton golf course and lost or ran to ground near Barton Grove. Rather nice gallop. Shamrock refused hedge and ditch.

Mrs Godman had nasty fall, her horse coming down over an ant heap galloping across Adlestrop Hill. Mrs Godman none the worse but saddle pummels smashed. A long day as I rode all the way to meet and got back at 5.30. Going on the plough in the morning perfectly awful. Bijou out for first time. *(Brassey, later married to Mr Arkwright, Master of N. Warwickshire).*

Deep going

"Consoled by mince pies brought me hot by Mrs Daly"

Friday, Jan. 19th

Moreton-in-Marsh. Rode Warrior, Mabel King John & Kate.

Found Cadley Arbour, ran through Batsford, back past Cadley Arbour, along side of hill, over the hill to Sezincote, across the vale past Donnington to Crawthornes, played about for some time and finally lost. I did not get the part from Sezincote to Donnington. Rather a twisty fox. Drew Sezincote covers blank. Found Bourton Wood and went away Dovedale end, turned left-handed past Troopers Lodge, close to Springhill, nearly to Hornsleasow and lost. Fox jumped up on the way home and they ran about Sezincote Warren for some time. Scent was then very good but they could not get the fox away.

Monday, Jan. 22nd

Boulter's Barn. Rode Shamrock.

Out entirely alone for the first time. Shamrock went a little short all day but came home sound. Found Sarsgrove and ran out past Jubilee Plantation and lost. Found and killed in Churchill Heath, (a large fox stronghold, south of Kingham Station, ploughed up in the sixties). Went away after another fox and ran well to the Norrels and out the other side but soon lost. No scent on the plough. Found and ran round about Bruern and Bould Wood for a long time and finally killed.

Rode Shamrock in a spur; found it fairly useful and did no damage to his side!

out entirely alone for first time

Captain Daly lets a little of his temper go on Mr Crowdie

Wednesday, Jan. 24th

Blockley. N. Cotswold. Rode Warrior.

Found Northwick Park and ran nearly to Campden Station where they lost. Most awkward country — all either wire, unjumpable ditches, or railway.

Found in Dovedale, ran into Bourton Wood and about and finally got away to Sezincote Warren, near where I left them as Warrior was only to have a short day. He was a little inclined to go short behind.

Friday, Jan. 26th

Bourton-on-the-Water. Rode Shamrock.

Clapton Gorse blank. Found in field near Sherborne Cow Pastures. Hounds ran straight across river for Rissington, turned right-handed and through Barrington Park, through Westwell Poor Lots, when Sturman caught them up, through Windrush Poor Lots to Bradwell Grove, ran about there for some time and finally killed. Hounds were entirely alone from Cow Pastures to Westwell Poor Lots, because we had to go round by New Bridge in order to cross the river. A great many people never found the hounds again. Drew Sherborne Cow Pastures blank and went home. Mabel tried horse of Mr Ormrod's but did not like him. Shamrock not very sound but went very well with help of spur.

Saturday, Jan. 27th

Ascot-under-Wychwood. Rode Warrior, Mabel King John.

Lovely day for riding about but did not find till about 3 o'clock in Tangley, when I went home as Warrior was only doing a half day. *(A long half day, since she must have left home at 9.30am and cannot have been back before 4pm!)*

Wednesday, Jan. 31st

Adlestrop. Rode Warrior, Mabel King John.

Found Oddington Ashes, ran through Upper Ashes and Maugersbury Grove; muddled about and lost. I came home then as I wanted Warrior on Friday, Shamrock being lame.

Friday, Feb. 2nd

Moreton-in-Marsh. Rode Warrior, Mabel tried Guy of Kingham's grey horse and rather liked it but a bit slow. Mother came out late on Spider.

Frogmore, Crawthornes and Fishpond Coppice blank. Fox jumped up in field above Donnington, ran past Crawthornes to Wolford Wood, muddled about and lost. I came home then as Warrior is only to do half days for the present. Rather a poor day.

Friday, Feb. 16th

Barrington New Inn. Rode Warrior, Mother out for a little on Spider but she was not strong enough to stay out long.

Marmion was shot on Feb. 4th.

Joy to be hunting again after fortnight's frost.

Found Westwell Poor Lots and ran to ground in drain close to Barrington Park by Dodd's Mill, through Sherborne Cow Pastures again, crossed river, through Great Rissington and lost somewhere about Tangley. Not an enjoyable run and the going perfectly awful. Again had to go a long way round when hounds crossed river and did not catch hounds for some time. A bridge ought to be built. *(This was done in the sixties by Desmond Godman, who was then farming Great Rissington Manor and Broadmoor as one farm).*

Warrior pulling rather badly.

Monday, Feb. 19th

Chapel House. Rode Shamrock, then Warrior. Mabel Johnnie.

Found at once in Walk Gorse and ran as hard as we could go to ground in ravine just beyond Pomfret Castle. About a 3-mile point in 12½ minutes. Very nice indeed; Shamrock went well. Found again in Walk Gorse, ran across railway and by Badger's Gorse, through some Heythrop covers, then left-handed nearly to Tew and lost. I stopped after Badger's Gorse as Shamrock had had enough, not having been out for three weeks. He was not very sound, poor boy.

Got on Warrior at Walk Gorse. Drew Salford blank; found Adlestrop Hill, ran past Cornwell to Mr Young's Homes. *(Now called Kingham Hill School).* Muddled about and finally killed just above Daylesford House.

Wedding guests at Guiting Grange.

Margaret Waddingham, family and guests.

Sleighing

Friday, Feb. 23rd

New Barn. Rode Warrior, Mabel King John.

Snowy morning; about an inch at least of snow on the ground. Very few people at the meet. Found close to Lodge Park and ran a little but could not make much of it and lost near Northleach Fever Hospital. Very slippery because it balled. Found Lodge Park and had a very nice fast little gallop. Drew Sherborne Cow Pastures and Osiers and covers about Sherborne blank. Thought I had better not keep Warrior out longer so went home. More people came out in the afternoon but it was most frightfully cold, though the snow went. Hounds found Farmington Grove and ran nearly to Lodge Park where they were stopped in order to catch special. Field a little annoyed I believe. *(It was customary to take hounds, and horses, on by train to Bourton-on-the-Water for meets on that side of the county).*

Monday, Feb. 26th

Pomfret Castle. Rode Shamrock, Mabel Kate.

Did not find until about 2 o'clock when fox was halloaed near Hawk Hill. Ran very well for about an hour and 20 minutes; to ground. Don't know where they ran but it was in the vale and we crossed a brook twice.

Muck SPREADING
There was 9 yards between heaps & between rows of heaps of manure

The first time we had either to jump over or in and out; Shamrock refused to jump over but jumped in and out very well. Kate jumped over very well. I got most of the run quite nicely and Shamrock went very well. He was very nearly sound. We did not get home till 6 o'clock. I was dead tired as we had ridden the whole way. (She must have left home at 9.00 to reach Pomfret Castle by 11.00).

Tuesday, Feb. 27th

Merrymouth. Rode Warrior, Mabel King John, Mother started on Spider but went home because of rain.

I came out rather late in order to have only half a day as I wanted Warrior again on Friday. Found the hounds at Bould Wood to which they had run very well from Tangley. King John very lame behind so Mabel had to take him home. Found Gawcomb and ran over the hill to Wyck Rissington, up through Wyck Hill to Gawcomb and out towards Little Rissington and lost. Very slow except first part to Wyck Rissington. Found Icomb Cow Pastures and ran very fast and killed on the banks of the Gawcomb Brook near Bledington. I kept on the outside all the way so did not see it. Drew Icomb Cow Pastures again, blank, and went home. Quite an enjoyable day. King John very lame indeed; strained his stifle very badly.

Out from 10

Friday, March 2nd

Stow-on-the-Wold. Rode Warrior and Shamrock. Mabel tried Mr Whitaker's Bay *(of Pudlicote)* and had Kate brought out.

Drew Slaughter Copses and Copse Hill blank. Found in Capt. Brassey's new covers and ran very fast to ground in a drain close to Wyck Rissington. Very nice gallop but short; not very many people got it. Changed on to Shamrock, who was going fairly sound on the grass but badly on the road. Fox halloaed near Brag's farm but we could not make much of it. Did not find again.

To 7 having
ridden from Stow
to Bradwell
Grove and back

Wednesday, March 7th

Bradwell Grove. Rode Shamrock.

A very bad day. A hot sun and dry wind made the scent very bad. Killed a fox in Bradwell Grove. Only found one other during the day. I was out from about 10 till 7 and rode the whole way. Shamrock very fairly sound.

Friday, March 9th

Evenlode. Rode Warrior, Mabel Kate.

Found and killed in Evenlode Mains. Found on Adlestrop Hill and ran up and down, round about for a long time but could never get away in the vale, probably on account of strong north-west wind. Found in Harcombs and ran onto Adlestrop Hill and lost. Found in Oddington Ashes and ran out towards Bledington, turned left-handed across Evenlode Brook, which we forded and at which Warrior came down on his front getting up steep bank on the far side but managed to get up; crossed close to junction and checked; fox halloaed and ran up nearly to Churchill, turned left-handed across Banbury line, passed Mr Young's Homes and to ground in Oddington Ashes. They ran very well some of the time. Warrior went most beautifully. He stubbed his knee somewhere.

Warrior on knees
going up steep Bank

Monday, March 12th

Troopers Lodge. (N. Cotswold). Rode Shamrock, Mabel her new horse.

Most frightfully cold north wind. Thought the meet was 11 but found it was 12 so had to wait for an hour at meet! Spent whole day nearly running about Bourton Wood and was perished with cold. Wish I had not gone out. Shamrock came home lame and could hardly move in his box next morning. Hateful day.

Friday, March 16th

Moreton. Rode Mrs Daly's Nun.

Frogmore blank. Found Crawthornes, ran nearly to Moreton racecourse, *(this was just south of Moreton on both sides of the Fosse Way)*, turned right-handed and followed the Evenlode to Stock Bridge, then to Broadwell Hill covers, and to ground in an earth bank of the Caudle ditch, just below our bottom fields. The Nun refused two ditches with me to begin with and then went beautifully. Quite a nice run. Crabby, Donnington and Banks Fee blank. Found in a Sezincote cover and ran across a rather big vale, through Batsford and lost in Bourton Wood. The piece from Sezincote to Batsford was very nice — Bijou and Zara Yollock took their own lines and went like birds. I followed humbly. Thoroughly enjoyed my day and my mount. *(Zara Pollock was Bijou Brassey's cousin, their mothers being sisters, and lived in Ireland. She later married the man who was to become famous as Lord Gowrie, V.C.)*.

Monday, March 19th

Chapel House. (Collection for Agric. Ben. Ass.) Rode Warrior, Mabel Baldoyle.

Walk Gorse blank!! Also Salford Osiers. Found Adlestrop Hill but could not do much. Evenlode Mains and Harcombs blank. Hounds went home only having found one fox all day. I got an awful scolding for keeping Warrior out all day.

Bijou & Zara jumping like Birds
(across the Sezincote Vale)

Friday, March 23rd

Farmington Grove. Rode Warrior, Mabel Baldoyle & Kate.

Farmington Grove blank. Then drew some of the Sherborne covers, also blank. Lodge Park blank. Halloaed on to a fox close to Lodge Park and ran more or less to Bibury and lost. Found in larch plantation just inside Sherborne Park, and ran well for about three fields towards Lodge Park, but then could make little more of it. Scent very bad; hot dusty day.

Monday, March 26th

Pomfret Castle. Rode De Wet, Mabel Rex (both Mrs Daly's).

Found in one of the yew covers but could do very little and soon lost. Found in Worton Heath in a hail storm, ran out at the bottom and up over the hill, turned left-handed below Worton and soon lost. Drew some of Heythrop blank and went home. Frightfully cold with snow and hail storms.

Wednesday, March 28th

Chipping Norton Junc. (Collection for Hunt Servants' Benefit Association). Rode Warrior, Mabel Baldoyle.

Got a dreadfull scolding for keeping warrior out all day

Icomb Cow Pastures blank. Gawcomb and Wyck Hill also blank. Halloaed onto fox while drawing Stow Bridge Copse. We galloped up through Wyck Hill to Maugersbury Grove, when the hounds got onto him and ran very fast to ground close to Oddington Upper Ashes — most disappointing as they really seemed like running.

Found Oddington Ashes and ran out the Gawcomb side as far as the line, turned up it right-handed for about 5 fields, turned sharp back and killed in a ditch. Delightful while it lasted, which was not more than about 5 minutes. Fox halloaed back into Oddington Ashes but hounds never got very near him and could not make much of it and finally gave it up at Daylesford.

Monday, April 2nd

Boulter's Barn. Rode Mr Pritchard's 'Lorna Doone' (of Donnington Manor), Mabel Baldoyle.

Found Sarsgrove and lost almost immediately. Jubilee Plantation and the Norrels blank.
Found Churchill Heath and ran through Bould Wood up past Idbury and lost in Tangley. Hounds went home. Hot, dry, windy day. Scent fairly good in the vale but very bad on the top. Lorna Doone a most delicious ride but just a little babyish in her jumping.

Mrs. Foster Mellior refreshed us

Wednesday, April 4th

Barton Gate. Stayed at Heythrop. Rode Warrior.

Found in a Barton Abbey cover and ran to ground very quickly. Drew several covers blank till we got to North Aston when Mr Foster Mellor refreshed us all with food and drink. We then drew Mr Foster Mellor's pet cover where there were four foxes, one of which was killed in the cover. Went away on another running well for a few fields but quickly lost. Fox halloaed while drawing Worton Heath, but hounds could make nothing of it. Very hot, dry day. My last day this season. Ground getting very hard.

---

49 days regular hunting, 2 days cubbing.

Warrior out 26 times. Shamrock out 21 times.

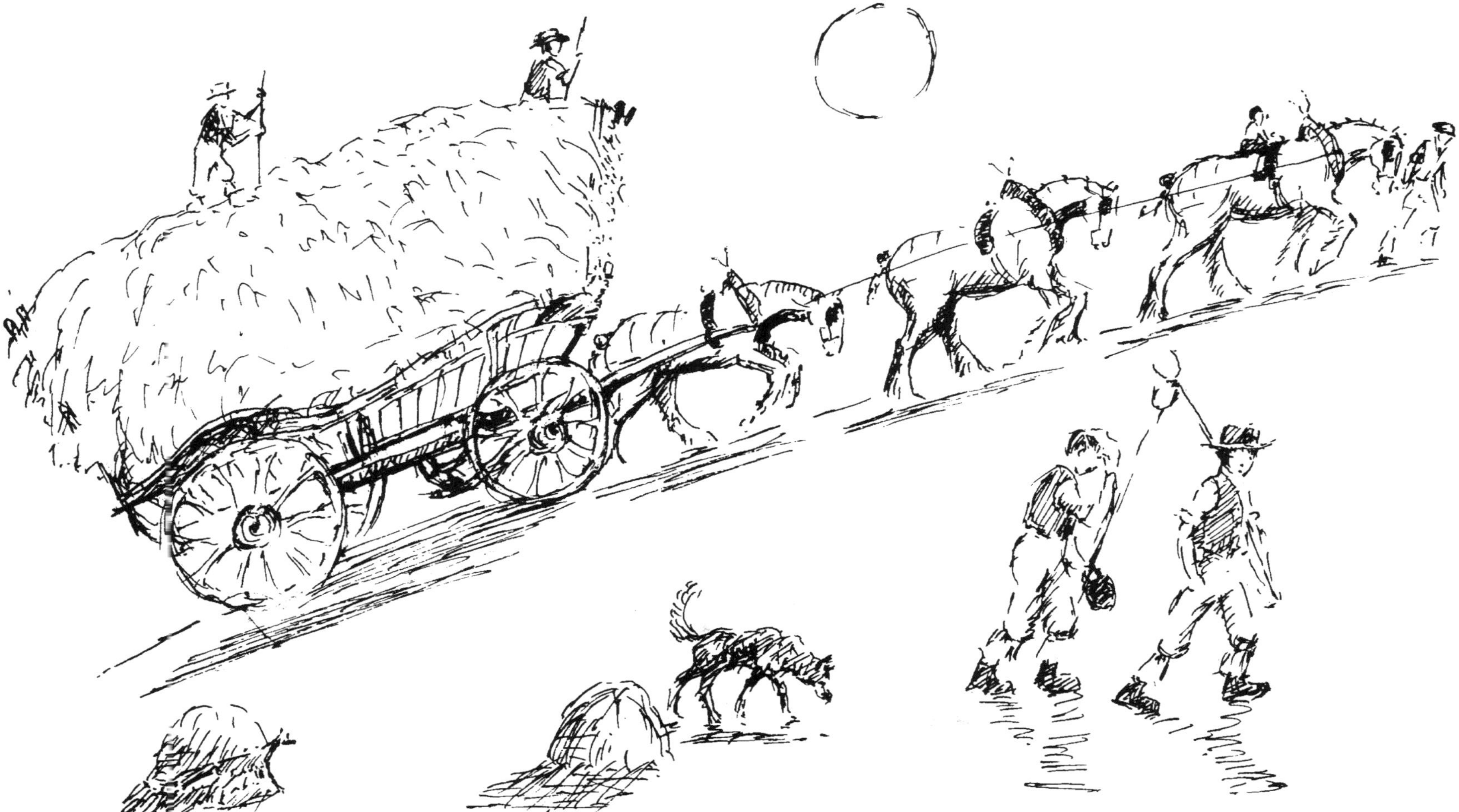

SUMMER 1906

HUNTING SEASON 1906-1907.

Bijou in tearing spirits talking of her engagement etc.

Wednesday, Sept. 19th

Foxholes. Rode my new horse Scout. Meet at 6.00.

I did not get to the hounds till 7.30. They killed a brace of cubs. It was delightful riding about, but the ground was like iron and the sky cloudless. The scent was not bad considering, and they were making a nice noise. Scout did his very best to get me off. It was just luck that he did not. I have never been on such an animal to kick and buck.

Monday, Oct. 1st

Oddington Ashes. Rode Warrior, who was very fresh and well.

The ground still like iron, but the scent wonderfully good. They killed 3 cubs. Mr Brassey and Col. Little were out. *(Col. Little was married to Iris (Dowie) Brassey).*

Friday, Oct. 5th

Bourton Wood. Rode Scout.

Plenty of foxes but the scent bad in the wood. I think they killed 2 cubs.

I saw Bijou (Brassey) out for the first time this season. She is in tearing spirits and delightful to talk to about her engagement, etc. *(to Mr Arkwright of the N. Warwickshire).*

Friday, Oct. 12th

Broadwell. 7 o'clock. Rode Warrior who has just been clipped and looks so well.

They had a bit of a gallop from Crawthornes before I arrived, but lost their fox. They found again thereabouts but did not do much. They also found in Frogmore and I think they killed. They found in Banks Fee covers and did not get away for some time, but finally got away below Donnington and ran across the vale quite nicely to Sezincote and I think lost. They killed, I think, a brace of cubs.

The going was excellent, but the country fearfully blind. Warrior pulled a good deal; he stuck his head up in the air and on one side. There were quite a lot of people out and it was a most enjoyable day.

Saturday, Oct. 13th

Stockley (Swinbrook). Rode Scout.

Found the hounds soon after 9 o'clock at Widley. They had already killed one cub. They ran one to ground in Widley and also found in covers round about Shipton but did not do anything. The morning was bright but with a very cold north wind, which caused the Scout to jump about in the most unseating manner. I heard that 17 brace had been killed already this season.

Monday, Oct. 15th

Campden (N. Cotswold). Rode Warrior.

Found the hounds at Churchill about 9.30. They found there and ran out towards Bourton Wood, without either us or their huntsman and Master, Sir John Campbell. We spent a long time riding about collecting them and then drew Churchill again, blank, after which they went to draw Sedgecomb and I went home. Warrior was a little more sane and did not throw his head about so much, but he was very heating on a hot morning. They killed one cub.

Wednesday, Oct. 17th

Gawcomb. Rode Scout.

Found in Gawcomb and ran about and above Maugersbury Grove and to ground and killed at Icomb Place. I had to come home just as they found at Wyck Hill, but I heard that they did not do much with that fox. They found at Icomb Cow Pastures and had a very nice run over the Oddington Vale, which must have been terrifyingly blind, and killed in Stow close to the cemetery.

Scout got into a ditch on the nearside of hedge. It gave way so we got out safely on the far side

Thursday, Oct. 18th

Kineton Thorns. 8 o'clock. N. Cotswold. Rode Scout.

The hounds never came to the meet but went straight to Trafalgar, where I had the greatest difficulty in finding them on account of the fog. They had run a fox to ground before I got to them. They found another and ran about Trafalgar for a long time and finally got him out to Condicote where he got into a drain, from which they bolted him and escaping the hounds he ran back to Rook's Pool Plantation and to ground, whence they dug him out and killed him. They found in Guiting Quarries and ran through Trafalgar and lost him. Not much scent and very foggy early, and bright and sunny later. Scout does not like big walls. He quite got the better of me over one, to my great annoyance. The North Cotswold have killed about 18 brace

" Scout stiff

Friday, Oct. 19th

Bourton Bridge. 8 o'clock. Rode Warrior, Mabel Baldoyle and Mother Bogy.

They did not draw Redesdale's Gorse but went straight to Aston Grove, where they found at once and killed about 3 fields away. Another fox went back into the Grove but they could not make anything of him. They found again in Mr Moss's cover and killed him. *(Mr Moss lived at Leygore, Judith's Grove was named after his daughter).* There were about 3 foxes in Farmington Grove but no scent. The scent was bad altogether but hopeless in the Grove. A lovely sunny day. Warrior was an angel; Baldoyle rather rampagious, and Bogy refused to jump walls.

Wednesday, Oct. 24th

Tangley. Rode Warrior, Mabel tried new horse, Mr Byard's of Cheltenham, and liked him. Mother rode Bogy.

We were in Tangley and Taynton Quarries all the morning. There were foxes but a very bad scent and we could do nothing with them. Zara Pollock was out and very pleasant and conversational.

We compared notes upon how very much we should miss Bijou. I think Zara will be at Heythrop more or less till Christmas.

Mother got Bogy to jump all right. The horse Mabel tried, and which has now been bought, is a big long tailed horse up to an unnecessary amount of weight, but jumps well and is fast. His price was £85.

Friday, Oct. 26th

Moreton. 8 o'clock. Rode Scout, Mabel Baldoyle.

Found and chopped a fox in Cadley Arbour. Ran another a field or two and lost him. During this bit Mabel met the ground — Baldoyle was frightfully fresh and fussy and as he was sidling around he crossed his hind legs and fell over on to his side. They were neither any the worse, but it has made us decide he is not fit for Mabel to ride and he is to be sold as soon as possible. He was quite mad and even a gallop round and round a ploughed field had no effect. There were foxes in Bourton Wood, but we could do nothing with them. Five foxes went away from one of the Sezincote covers near Sezincote Warren, and they ran one of them down to near Sezincote House and lost. We drew Blackthorns blank, and then went home. I had not a single thing to jump. It was a pleasant cool morning but not much scent.

Saturday, Oct. 27th

Tangley. Rode Warrior. Mother came out for a short time on Bogy.

I was punished for laziness in starting, for before I arrived they had found in Tangley and run to Bruern and lost. They found again in Tangley and raced about the cover on a very good scent but finally lost. They drew the Rissington Common covers blank but found in a small cover between Little Rissington and Wyck and soon killed him. They found again in a very small cover just above Little Rissington and ran out as far as the Barrington road and back to ground just below where they killed their first fox.

It was nothing of a run but I enjoyed it hugely as I got away in front of other people and jumped 2 or 3 fences without a lead!

The Nun gave Capt. Daly a fall trying to double a hedge. She lamed herself but did him no harm. A most lovely bright sunny day but there had been some rain during the night, which, I suppose, accounted for the scent.

They have killed 22 brace in 23 days this cubbing season.

12 days cubbing.
Warrior 6. Scout 6.

Monday, Oct. 29th

Heythrop. Opening meet. Rode Scout, Mabel Mrs Daly's Rex, Mother Bogy.

Found at once close to the house and were running more or less till about 2 o'clock, about Heythrop, Walk Gorse, Badger's Gorse and Rollright. I then left them and went to Over Norton to wait for Mabel. They had another rather pleasant gallop, but did not kill. It was a good day for the opening meet. It was a very cold day and the scent fair. Scout is quite nice and fast and a delightful ride, but he does not jump very clean and he likes a lead. Peggy took a voluntary. She was riding The Duke and he hit some rails very hard and sent Peggy off on the off side. *(Peggy Fenwick came from Abbotswood. She married Mr Vere Chaplin, nephew of the celebrated 'Squire' Chaplin.)*

Friday, Nov. 2nd

Stow-on-the-Wold. Rode Scout, Mabel tried a Byard horse and then rode her new horse. Mother rode Bogy.

Scout was quite dangerously fresh, as he was kicking and bucking in the road on the way to the draw. They found in Slaughter Copses and ran by Quar Wood to Maugersbury and killed in Stow by Enoch's Tower. No one was with them as they slipped very quietly away across the brook, which we had difficulty in finding a way over. Drew Copse Hill blank; found in Capt. Brassey's covers above Slaughter and ran down through Lower Slaughter, through Copse Hill, Upper Slaughter and to ground near where found. Found another fox close by and after much difficulty got him away through Lower Slaughter and killed just the other side of Bourton Bridge. Jumped a hedge with a blind ditch on the near side, which Scout went into, but owing to the hedge giving way, got out safely on the far side. Found and killed two foxes in Eyford and went away with another and had quite a nice little spurt over the walls nearly to Lower Swell and to Copse Hill, where I left them. It was a very hard day on horses as there were so many banks. Scout refused some walls but jumped others very well. Mr Byard was riding Baldoyle and got his hind leg very badly cut in a hole in a bridge. Mr Renfrew *(the Broadway vet.)*, was wired for. He says it is very serious and he does not know whether he will get over it. Mr Byard was riding him to see if he would buy him. Scout went home sound but is very stiff behind this morning. It was a lovely sunny day with quite a good scent.

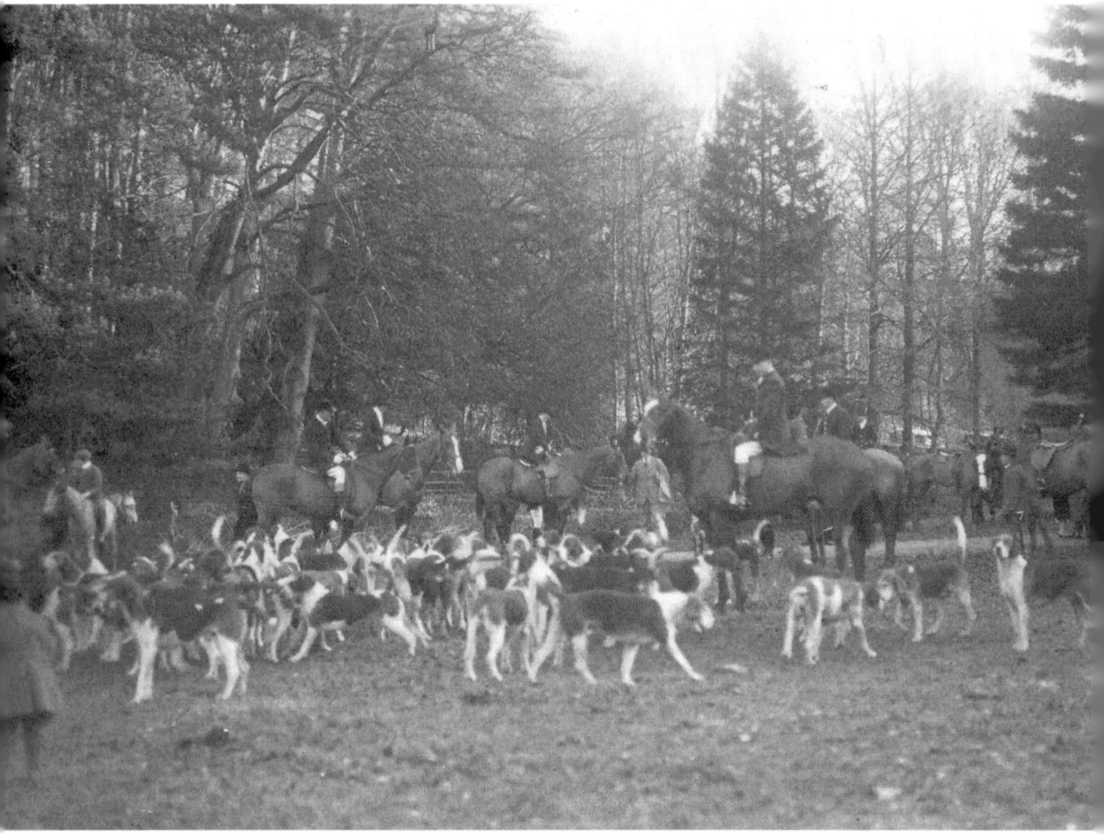

Meet at Eyford Lodge.

Fosse Cottage during the First World War.

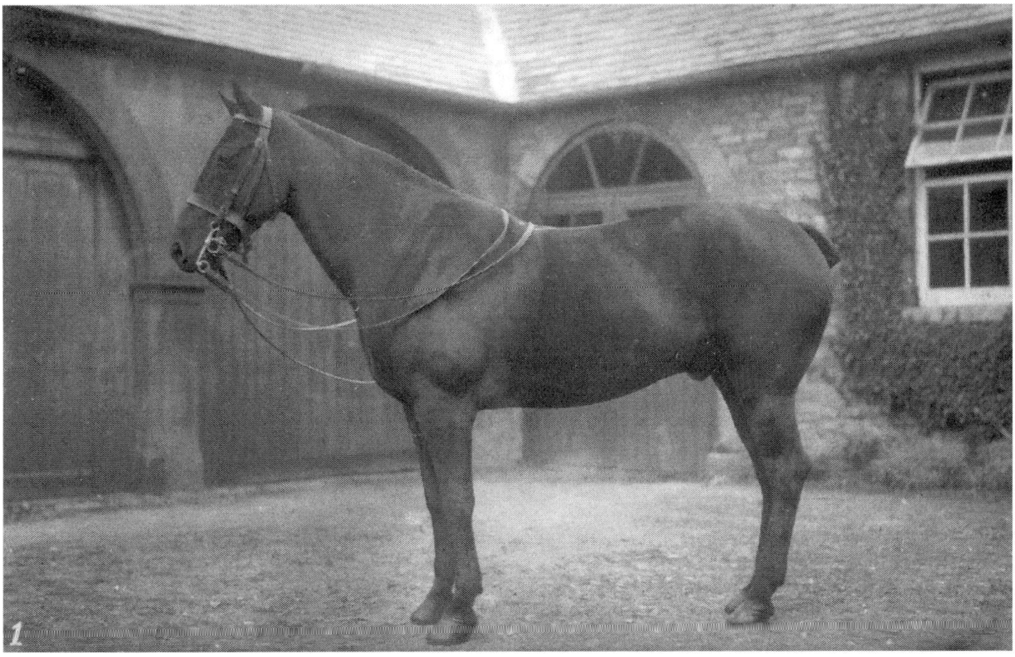

Stables at Eyford Park.

Monday, Nov. 5th

Boulter's Barn. Rode Warrior, Mabel her new horse.

We spent hours running round Sarsgrove and finally killed 2 and went away on a third nearly to Heythrop and lost. Drew the Norrels blank. Found plenty of foxes in Churchill Heath but could do nothing. A lovely day, but scent very bad. Did not get home till 6 o'clock.

Baldoyle got his leg cut getting it in hole in Bridge

Wednesday, Nov. 7th

Adderbury. Rode the Nun & Rex.
Stayed at Over Norton.

Drove with Capt. Daly to the meet, 13 miles in 5 minutes under the hour *(i.e. 14 m.p.h., presumably in a gig. On a covert or galloping hack one expected to go to the meet at between 12-14 m.p.h.)*. Found and ran to ground and killed close to the meet. Found again close to meet and ran to ground. Halloaed on to fox and ran through Wilson's Gorse, close to Deddington, turned right-handed and finally killed in Mr Stilgoe's farm buildings; about 40 minutes, quite nice. Found a fox in turnip field close to where we had killed, in Bicester country, and ran fast for 20 minutes and to ground. Returned to Adderbury to eat the fox which went to ground in the morning. Bolted another out of same drain and ran it to ground in 2 fields, dug him out and ate him. Sturman had his hand rather badly bitten by the fox, so the hounds went home early, and my second horse Rex was no use. A good scent on the whole, but occasionally spoilt by threatening storms.

Vet wired for.

elt very grand coming with Mr Brassey
nd Capt. Brassey on The Special
NOTGROVE

Friday, Nov. 9th

New Barn. Rode Warrior, Mabel her new horse.

Felt very grand coming with Mr Brassey and Capt. Daly and the Special from Chipping Norton. An awful day, raining and blowing and very cold. About 1¾ inches of rain in last 24 hours and the floods out at the junction. Sturman was not out owing to the fox bite of Wednesday, so Will Lockey hunted the hounds. Lodge Park blank, found in Broad Field but could do nothing in the wind and storm. Found and killed another close by. Another one went away from the same cover and the hounds were got on to him; there was no scent and we soon lost him. Did not find again till we got to the Sherborne covers, where we left them trying to get the fox out of a small larch cover. We waited for nearly an hour but they seemed no nearer getting him out. Baldoyle is going on very well. Scout is not to come out for another week.

Monday, Nov. 12th

Pomfret Castle. Rode the Nun, Mabel Rex.

Badger's Gorse blank. Found Tew Pond Tail and ran out a short way towards Heythrop, turned right-handed, crossed the road by Pomfret Castle and lost.

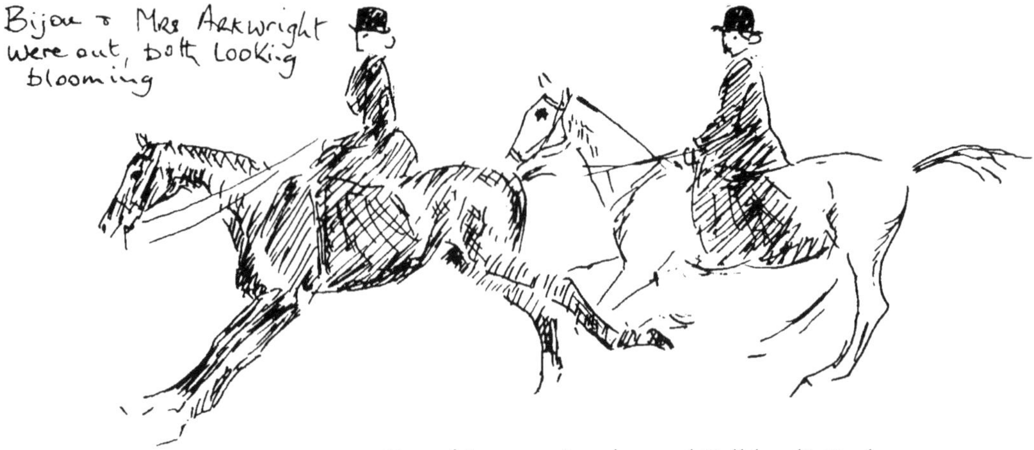
Bijou & Mrs Arkwright were out, both looking blooming

"Capt. Daly sent us home"

Found in gorse just beyond Falkland's Bushes ran up over the hill and through some Tew covers, turned right-handed and crossed the Chipping Norton — Deddington road and down the hill, turned right-handed along the bottom and then right-handed again up on to the hill and to ground on the Deddington — Chipping Norton road. This was a complete circle but very enjoyable for those who kept with the hounds. Found in French's Hollow, but soon lost. Found and killed in Iron Down. Found in gorse on Hawk Hill and ran across Deddington — Chipping Norton road and some way on, then turned back and by Hawk Hill again and through some Tew covers, then right-handed across the Deddington road again, where Capt. Daly sent us home. He told us when he got back that they had done the same circle over again and then gave up.

Mabel and I enjoyed our day and our mounts very much. Bijou and Mr Arkwright were out, both looking blooming. We did not get home till 7.30, but mother was quite placid. The scent was good. There were crowds of strange women out, who were very helpless and got in the way. Sturman was out again.

Wednesday, Nov. 14th

Chipping Norton Junction. Rode Scout, Mabel Lancer (the Cold Aston horse).

Bruern blank. Found too many foxes in Bould Wood and spent hours there.

Home 7.30: Mother quite placid

Went to Gawcomb where we found too many foxes again and dashed about Gawcomb and finally killed one. Drew Icomb Cow Pastures blank and hounds went home. It was rather nice weather and the scent was not very bad, but the foxes were.

Warrior was very unmanageable again, as he would throw his head up in the air whenever I tried to stop him.

"Lots of strange women, helpless & getting in the way".

Friday, Nov. 16th

Moreton. Rode Scout, Mabel Yeoman.

Found and killed in Crawthornes. Found and killed in Crab Orchard. Donnington and Banks Fee blank. Found in larch cover near Sezincote Warren and ran into the Warren and back again, then across the Stow — Broadway road nearly to the Sezincote lane, turned back across the road again and towards Sezincote Warren. We then came home as neither of our horses wanted a long day. A pouring wet day — most depressing — Scout very fresh. Scent fairly good.

Thursday, Nov. 15th

Temple Guiting. N. Cotswold. Mounted by Mr Pritchard on Lorna Doone.

A wet day and a bad day. Found in Lee Wood, ran about for a bit and finally got out to Guiting Brake. Kineton Thorns blank. Found Trafalgar, but no scent and soon lost. I enjoyed my day very much as Lorna Doone is such a darling.

Warrior jumping Big Wall

Monday, Nov. 19th

Chapel House. Rode Warrior, Mabel Lancer & Yeoman.

I was going to have Scout out too but he was stiff again behind after Friday. Walk Gorse blank! Found in gorse just above Salford Osiers, ran into Over Norton village and then out as far as the Banbury Lodge, Heythrop, but I don't think the hounds owned to him after Over Norton. Found in Salford Osiers, ran left-handed down the vale and across the Boulter's Barn road nearly to the Sarsden level crossing, turned to the left across railway and brook up to Mr Young's Homes. They could not make much of it after this, though the fox was seen back across the line by Sarsden level crossing. Sturman cast on for some time, but finally gave it up. I went home, as it was about enough for one horse, the ground being so very heavy. Warrior went very well, but got his head up most fearfully. We jumped a gate all by ourselves! It was a cold day and the scent fairly good. It looks like freezing and there was snow on the ground in the morning.

Thursday, Nov. 22nd

Broadway. N. Cotswold. Rode Scout, who seemed to go rather shuffly and not to feel very fit.

I motored to the meet with Peggy. Found in Middle Hill and after a good deal of messing about, got away as far as Weston Park and lost. We spent a long time in Weston Park doing practically nothing. Sir John Campbell never seems to hurry himself, but lounges slackly about; he certainly leaves the hounds to themselves quite enough, rather too much I should think. Having at last given up the fox in Weston Park, we trotted off to Lidcomb Wood where we found, and the hounds ran part of the way down the hill into the vale, while we stood at the top watching them hunting most beautifully all by themselves. There seemed no chance of them getting away from the side of the hill and it was 3.30 so I went home.

It was a lovely sunny day,
delightful for riding about and not a bad scent. Scout was, as I expected, generally stiff all over next morning, so we sent for Renfrew, who has prescribed a fortnight's rest. I am afraid Scout is not going to be a very sound horse.

"Lorna Doone such a darling"

Friday, Nov. 23rd

Merrymouth. Rode Warrior.

Mr Byass *(of Wyck Hill, and whose grandson Francie married in 1910.)*, was out again after being laid up with a cold for about 3 weeks. Mrs Brassey made her second appearance this season — at least the opening meet is the only other time I have seen her. Mr Oakley was out and had to be congratulated on his engagement to Mrs Samuda's niece *(of Bruern Abbey)*. We found in Taynton Quarries, ran out across the Burford road and through Shipton Barrow, left-handed above Shipton and left again to Tangley and lost. Quite a nice little circle with lots of jumping over decidedly large walls with upright coping stones which Warrior jumped most beautifully. Found in Tangley, ran out a little way towards Barrington but soon lost. There were too many hares about. Capt. Daly now offered Mabel and me our mounts for Monday which filled me with joy. We had just finished drawing Tangley when hounds were halloaed on to a fox, ran very nicely down into Bould Wood and out the other side, through Bruern and into Milton village, then turned right-handed up to Fifield where he was seen and headed back towards Bould Wood. The hounds were cast back into Bould Wood and I came home, as it was enough for one horse, the weather being hot and sunny and the ground very heavy. It was quite a nice run though not very fast. Warrior went beautifully. Zara had Emperor out, his first appearance at a Friday meet. He went most awfully well. I wish Warrior were anything like as fast.

Warrior Pulling

We jumped a gate all by ourselves

Monday, Nov. 26th

Great Tew. Rode the Nun, Mabel De Wet.

Found in Tew Park and ran very fast, most of the way along a road, to Sandford Park, checked, then turned left-handed through Ledwell village and to ground by the roadside just beyond. Found in Worton Heath and ran to Barton where we hung about for a bit, then got away on the far side; ran as hard as they could up by the side of the Dorn as far as Rousham Gap, then turned sharp left-handed, and back again to ground in Barton Wood. We then got our orders for home. There was a very good scent, and the last bit was just as fast as we could gallop. Mabel and I were well up in the last bit, but did not see anything of the piece from Worton Heath to Barton; I think only Sturman and one other did see it. We were a little afraid it was not going to do for hunting, as until just before 11 o'clock there was a dense fog. We both loved our mounts. There was not much jumping however.

Wednesday, Nov. 28th

Stow Station. Rode Warrior, Mabel Lancer. Mother came out for a short time on Spider.

Found at once in Stow Bridge Copse, ran to the right of Wyck Rissington and about half way to Little Rissington, turned left-handed up the hill to Gawcomb, through Gawcomb and out the Westcote end, down into the vale in the direction of Bould Wood, turned left-handed, crossed

the Gawcomb ditch, Passed Icomb Cow Pastures, above Oddington Upper Ashes, by Ash Farm and to Maugersbury Grove, where I came home as they got on to a fresh fox and I thought Warrior had had about enough. It was a real good, very fast hunt and with very few checks. From Maugersbury Grove they went away on a fresh fox, through Upper Ashes, past Jeffreys's farm and finally lost just the other side of Churchill Heath. They came back and drew Oddington Ashes where they found, ran out by the Spotted Pig (the pub below Oddington windmill), below Maugersbury, nearly to Botany Bay, turned back through Maugersbury Grove and killed close to the railway bridge below the Spotted Pig.

This makes almost a record day. People were saying that they had never had such a good day with the Heythrop. The day was bright and sunny and there was a wonderful scent. The hounds were making great music. I saw the last run on my feet. Warrior went most awfully well, really galloped on in a wonderful way. Zara, lucky girl, had two horses out, so got the whole thing. I don't think however that Emperor went very well in the morning. Captain Daly gave her the brush for going so well in the last run on Rex. Mrs Godman said she got jumped off her new horse, whom however she likes very much. Warrior got his hind legs into a ditch below Maugersbury Grove, entirely my fault though, as I did not send him at it fast enough.

May we have many more days like this. Scout is having a fortnight's rest.

Gawcombe Ditch

Friday, Nov. 30th

Farmington Grove. Rode Mr Garnett's Mullinger, Mabel Mr Garnett's Bachelor & Yeoman. *(Mr Garnett was Rector of Lower Swell and later officiated at Francie's wedding).*

Found in Farmington Grove, ran fast for a few fields towards Sherborne Cow Pastures, then checked and draggled on nearly to New Bridge and lost. Drew Sherborne Cow Pastures blank. Found in Farmington Grove ran fast to Farmington Pillars, turned back left-handed and killed just outside Farmington Kennel Plantation. Found in Aston Grove and I came home. Mullinger went very well in the little gallop we had, but was terrifying to ride in between as he stumbled so. I think I am too heavy for him. There was a fair scent. The weather was warm in the morning but turned cold later.

Warrior had had enough

Monday, Dec. 3rd

Boulter's Barn. Rode Warrior, Mabel Lancer.

Found in Sarsgrove, ran into the middle of Chipping Norton and lost. Drew Sarsgrove again and after dashing about it for some time got away by Churchill but could not make much of it, then cast on into the Norrels where there was a fox, but he turned back towards Sarsgrove and was eventually lost. They then drew the Partridge cover, where was found the hunted fox, and whom they killed in the cover. They drew the Jubilee Plantation blank and went home. I spent part of the day at the blacksmith's shop at Churchill, as Warrior lost a shoe and I had to go there to have him shod. Bijou was out, but not Mr Arkwright as he had had to go to his sister whose husband is very ill.

It was a stormy day, but at first the scent seemed rather good, but it failed later.

after very fast hunt across Gawcombe Vale

Wednesday, Dec. 5th

North Aston. Rode the Nun and stayed at Over Norton.

Found at Dean Hill, did a bit of a circle and to ground below North Aston close to the river. Found in some withies by the river, ran into Dean Hill, Zara coming a cropper on Isabel on the way there doing a bit of a dash on her own! Three foxes went to ground in Dean Hill. After a long time we got away on one, and went through North Aston, across the canal and railroad and into the Bicester country, draggling on a long time and possibly changing foxes. Had a long ride of about 15 miles back to Over Norton against an icy wind. It was a stormy day and the scent catchy. An enjoyable day with lots of jumping.

"Warrior down in a ditch"

Friday, Dec. 7th

Knowle. North Warwickshire. Rode Bijou's Rats and stayed at Hatton.

A very bad day and came home on account of fog.

Wednesday, Dec. 12th

Adlestrop. Rode Warrior, Mabel Lancer.

Day after Stow Ball, so lots of strangers out. Drew Mrs Thursby's covers blank *(Broadwell Hill)*. Found in Oddington Ashes; 3 foxes went away, the hounds after the one in the direction of Kingham, and most of the field after the one towards Bledington! No-one got away with the hounds and we found them run to ground near Kingham. Icomb Cow Pastures was apparently blank though they say there was a fox there, only they could not get him out as it was so thick. Found in Gawcomb, ran out below Icomb when a cold storm came on and did away with the scent, however we draggled on to Wyck Hill and then came home in a bitterly cold snow storm. I think the scent was good in the morning.

Muddy Back!

Monday, Dec. 17th

Chapel House. Rode Warrior, Mabel Lorna Doone whom mother has settled to buy from Mr Pritchard for £100.

Walk Gorse blank. Found in Salford Osiers, ran left-handed nearly to Cornwell, then turned right-handed up the hill past Daylesford House, right again over Adlestrop Hill on to Chastleton Hill where there was a check, owing I think to there being two foxes; struck the line by Chastleton, ran past Chastleton Grove nearly to Evenlode Mains where they turned short left-handed, ran into the Harcombs where we stayed looking for the fox, which I think went on — anyhow, we could not find him and had to give it up. Found just below Adlestrop Hill, ran a quick circle by Daylesford House and killed in a field between where they had found and the road up Adlestrop Hill. I then went home. It was a warm cloudy day and the scent was good. I did not get the first part of the run as far as Adlestrop Hill well, because Warrior came down in a boggy ditch about 3 fields from Salford Osiers. Captain Daly also came down in it. It was quite small but the bog was up level with the field and Warrior just jumped into the middle. I fear it has laid him up for at least 10 days as next morning he was lame, though he finished the day quite sound and went well. Mr Renfrew says he has sprained the muscles in his shoulder. There were a great many muddy backs, probably because the ground was so rotten after the frost.

Zara coming a Cropper cutting a bit of a dash

ll Brassey sons-in-law out except Mr. Arkwright

Mr Pritchard had a fall off Q.E.D. Rosie Daly made her first appearance on horseback this season. Mabel liked Lorna Doone and mother has bought her for £100.

Friday, Dec. 21st

Moreton. Rode Scout, Mabel Lorna Doone.

Found at Cadley Arbour, ran out at the bottom, turned left-handed up over the hill, through Batsford, out towards Bourton Wood; turned right-handed down into the vale, past Blockley Station and into the Warwickshire country; presently turned right again and went close under Batsford, under Sezincote, past Banks Fee, then turned left and ran to ground in the Longborough — Moreton road. It must have been a good run but I did not see it as I was nursing Scout as it was his first day and I did not attempt to really gallop him. They drew Banks Fee covers blank and went home. It was a day of accidents. Mabel broke her wrist catching a gate which someone in front missed and let swing. No more hunting for her for a month; and she was so delighted with Lorna Doone. Mr Garnett's Bachelor fell down in a field, rolled on him, and squashed him rather.

Mr Mills' horse fell down by the roadside, and Mr Mills put his shoulder out. Scout was most shockingly fresh and made himself a fearful nuisance to me and everyone else. It was a bitterly cold day with an east wind.

"Mr Garnet rolled on"

Monday, Dec. 24th

Pomfret Castle. Rode Mr Moon's Grey. *(Mr Moon was the Rector of Heythrop — the story is that he received a letter from the Duke of Beaufort offering him the living at Badminton on the same day as Mr Brassey offered him Heythrop, and he chose Heythrop).*

It was hardly fit to hunt on account of the frost, but got all right in the afternoon. They found a fox in a kale field, ran by Swerford House and out the other side where the fox was headed back past Swerford House again and to Badger's Gorse, then back again to Swerford House and to ground. Drew Tew Pond Tail blank. Found Cow Hill but soon lost. Drew Hawk Hill, gorse near Falkland's Bushes *(this gorse must be what we now call Hambidge's Gorse),* and Great Tew Gardens blank and went home. I liked the grey very much. All Mr Brassey's sons-in-law except Mr Arkwright were out.

Had a sad accident on the way home. I was hacking Scout and, trotting along near Adlestrop Station, he fell down in the middle of the road. He had a bad cut above the knee, a cut above the eye which had to be sewn up, the skin off the point of his shoulder and his thigh! He was horribly stiff next morning but is going on very well. It was the greatest piece of luck he did not break his knees. There was a week's frost and snow from Xmas to the New Year, then I burnt my head and was laid up for nearly three weeks.

§ This apparent non-sequitur, when she starts the day on Mr Moon's grey and hacks home on Scout, is exactly as written in the original.

Mabel broke her wrist on swinging gate

"Scout was most shockingly fresh"

Friday, Jan. 18th

Merrymouth. Rode Warrior & Scout, Mabel Lorna Doone.

Found in Tangley but there was no scent and we soon lost. Found in Barrington but again soon lost. Found many foxes in Bould Wood but could do nothing. A very bad day.
It was bright and sunny and there had been a frost the night before. George Hawker rode Scout to begin with, and he said he refused everything he came to. I got on him half way through the day, but unfortunately had nothing besides gaps to jump. Mabel's wrist stood the riding all right. It was exactly a month since she broke it.

Long ride of about 15 miles (home to stables)

Monday, Jan. 21st

Pomfret Castle. Rode Warrior.

Found in Badger's Gorse; ran very nicely as far as Swerford after which they could not make much more of it. Found in Tew Pond Tail; ran slowly with many checks through Badger's Gorse, Swerford and finally gave him up near Tew Pond Tail, when I came home. There was a better scent than on Friday.

FROST — — — — — —

Monday, Feb. 11th

Heythrop. Rode Scout who was horribly fresh.

The frost was not nearly out of the ground and a good many people slipped up. Found by the rockery and ran round and round the place for two hours, and killed a mangy fox in Peel's Gorse. I came home as they went to draw farther away.

Most of the field after one fox: Hounds after another one

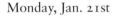

Warrior going Well

Tuesday, Feb. 12th

Chipping Norton Junction. Rode Warrior.

It had snowed and frozen in the night, but in the morning it turned to rain. The going was still rather bad. Found in Bould Wood; ran out by Fifield and the Merrymouth nearly to the Barrington lane and lost. Found in Bruern, ran out by Lyneham and into the Norrels and lost. Found in Churchill Heath and ran out to the left, up near Churchill, by the Norrels and lost by the Jubilee cover. Found in Sarsgrove, but could do no good.

Mrs Godman jumped off

Friday, Feb. 15th

Moreton. Rode Scout, Mabel Lorna Doone & Lancer.

Rook Hill and Aston Magna covers blank. Found in gorse below Cadley Arbour; ran a ring round below Batsford and into Bourton Wood, through Dovedale, above Northwick Park, through Blockley and back into Bourton Wood. Found in Thickleather, ran back again into Bourton Wood. I came home so as to bring Scout out again on Monday. Rotten day. Rode Scout in a spur and he went much better and did not kick so badly. He came down in a small ditch but neither were any the worse.

Saturday, Feb. 16th

Trooper's Lodge. N. Cotswold. Rode Warrior.

Found in Dovedale, ran back into Bourton Wood where remained some time and lost. Found in an osier bed outside Northwick Park; the fox swam across the lake, below Sedgecomb and to ground on the hill above Campden. Messed about after a halloa — Sedgecomb blank. Found in Northwick Park, ran a ring and lost. Found in Stayt's Gorse, ran a bit of a ring and lost by Churnell. Came home. A very bad day. Up and down hill all the time; Warrior pulling rather.

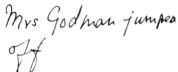

Monday, Feb. 18th

Chapel House. Rode Scout & Warrior, Mabel Lancer & Lorna Doone.

Found in Walk Gorse; ran towards Heythrop as far as the Banbury — Chipping Norton road and soon lost. Salford Osiers blank. Found on Adlestrop Hill; ran round below Chastleton Hill, turned right-handed over the hill and nearly to the railway bridge below Boulter's Barn and lost. The country about there is most frightfully wired. I jumped some wire through a weak place in a high fence and nearly came down, but was lucky to get off with only a few scratches. May Price *(another Brassey daughter)* cut her horse rather badly. I think I am going to love Scout. He was jumping very well. I changed on to Warrior before we drew Harcombs, where we found, ran very nicely to Adlestrop, over the railway by the station, where was the last we saw of the hounds till we found them run to ground between Evenlode and the Harcombs. We crossed the Evenlode by Adlestrop station and found ourselves on the wrong side, for the hounds recrossed the line and we had a fast and furious gallop alongside the river up to Stock Bridge, where we obtained news of the hounds and made the best of our way to where we found them run to ground. We had lots of jumping and were slightly consoled by knowing that nobody was with the hounds. There was a good scent in the vale but not much on the hill.

"Scout horribly fresh"

Slipping up on frosty ground

Thursday, Feb. 21st

Northleach. Rode Scout, Mabel Lorna Doone.

The horses were roughed *(frost nails)* to be able to get to the meet, but the going afterwards was all right. Drew several covers blank until we got to Lodge Park where we found and ran to Farmington Grove, messed about a good deal and lost. Sherborne covers blank, and Sherborne Cow Pastures blank. Fox was seen in the water meadows by the river, we draggled back nearly to Farmington Grove and lost.

The lake, Eyford.

Swiss Farm, Eyford.

Meet at the Unicorn, Stow-on-the-Wold.

Saturday, Feb. 23rd

Hornsleasow. North Cotswold. Rode Warrior, Mabel Lorna Doone.

The frost which stopped us hunting on Saturday was hardly out of the ground. Found in Hornsleasow covers, but could not do much. Found near Hornsleasow, ran into Lidcombe Wood and back. Only Mr Barnsly and the Master got this gallop as Sir John never let us know that he had gone away! We got to them when they had got back to Hornsleasow and from there they draggled on to Sezincote Warren where they marked him to ground. Found near Springhill, ran about a field and lost. Found in gorse by Springhill Lodges, ran across the Broadway road and lost. A bad day and Warrior was very trying, always throwing his head up.

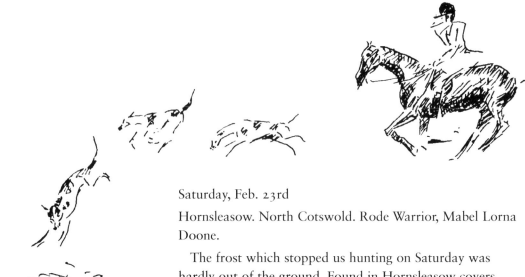

Wednesday, Feb. 27th

Bradwell Grove. Rode Scout.

Found in Bradwell Grove and made a big circle towards Alvescot and Burford and back again into Bradwell Grove where we spent some time, but at last got him away again and killed near Alvescot. Found in Patcat Gorse, ran to Bibury racecourse where we got mixed up with hares and lost. Drew gorse near Patcat blank and I came home. They had a very good run afterwards from Jolly's Gorse. More people out than I have ever seen — Scout took to the stone walls like a duck to water.

Friday, March 1st

Stow. Rode Warrior, Mabel Lorna Doone.

Slaughter Copses, Copse Hill and new larch covers blank. Covers above Swiss Cottage blank. Fox halloaed in direction of Slaughter but could make nothing of it. Some of the Eyford covers blank. Went to a halloa near Swell Wold, ran towards Pole Plantation, turned right-handed and down past Fir Farm into Kirkham meadow, turned right-handed up past Copse Hill, right-handed and into Fir Farm where he got onto the roof of a barn and after much trouble they chivvied him down and killed him. Abbotswood blank. Found in Pole Plantation, ran down past Abbotswood stables, across the Stow — Swell road, below Nether Swell Manor, past Slaughter Copses, turned right-handed up past Copse Hill, down past Swiss Cottage, right-handed into Slaughter where they lost. The bit in the vale from Swell to Slaughter was very nice. Scent fairly good. Collection for Royal Agricultural Ben. Ass.

Tuesday, March 5th

Wolford. Warwickshire. Rode Scout, Mabel Mr Pritchard's Gold Dust.

Found in Wolford Wood, ran round about and lost. Found in Dunsdon and quickly lost. Drew Aston Hailes and Todenham blank. Very bad scent, cold, rather wet.

Wednesday, March 6th

Boulter's Barn. Rode Warrior, Mabel Lorna Doone.

Found in Sarsgrove, ran out nearly to the Jubilee Plantation, turned back into Sarsgrove and out towards Churchill and soon lost. The rest of the Sarsden covers blank. Found in the Norrels. Ran out towards Ascott and lost. Found in Churchill Heath and lost near the Norrels. Bruern blank. Found in Bould Wood, ran out by Idbury, past the Merrymouth, through this end of Tangley and lost just short of the Barrington lane. Went home.

Friday, March 8th

Bourton-on-the-Water. Rode Scout.

Found in Clapton Gorse, ran nearly down to the brook, turned back past Clapton Gorse, just above Bourton Bridge and lost about the top of Whiteshoots Hill. Aston Grove blank. Found in Farmington Grove, ran very fast round and about and at last got away towards Bourton; turned left-handed by Clapton Gorse, up the hill and on towards Gilbert's grave, turned left-handed and back into Farmington Grove and finally lost. Sherborne Cow Pastures and other covers near blank. Mr Brassey's last day before starting for Japan — a most fearfully windy day and endless up and down hill. *(One is left wondering whether he went in his own yacht, and how long this journey took him?)*

Monday, March 11th

Heythrop. Rode Warrior, Mabel Lorna Doone.

Found in the Ovens, ran nearly to the Banbury Lodge, turned sharp back past the church, to the right of Heythrop House, past Enstone and killed just beyond Ditchley. About a 6-mile point, over very uninteresting country though. Found near Heythrop House, ran to ground close to the Enstone Lodge, dug him out and killed him. Drew Walk Gorse blank.

"Scout jumping Well"

Wednesday, March 13th

Gawcomb. Rode Scout.

Came down from London in the morning, so did not get to the junction till 12 o'clock and missed the first bit from Gawcomb, where they found at once. They ran straight down the vale to Bledington where I met them. They checked for some time, then got on the line and ran up the vale past Icomb Cow Pastures nearly up to Gawcomb House; then turned left-handed, ran straight down the vale, very fast to Bledington again and lost. I then came home as Scout hit his leg very hard on the latch of a gate and was going a bit lame. They had 2 more runs and finally killed their fox in the open close to Icomb Cow Pastures. A very good day.

"A Fast & Furious gallop"

Friday, March 16th

Moreton. Rode Warrior.

Frogmore, Crawthornes, Crabby and Fishponds blank. Foxes viewed in a field above Donnington, ran down towards Crawthornes, just crossed the Moreton road, then turned back past Fishpond Coppice, below Donnington, up through Banks Fee, just above Donnington Brewery, and to ground near Condicote. Very fast and pumping for horses. Found in Dibden's Gorse and ran to ground close to Sezincote House. Found in Thickleather, ran first pointing rather towards Batsford, then turned right-handed and got as far as the Moreton road between Moreton and the racecourse, turned sharp back and killed below Batsford.

A good day. Rather windy, but warm.

Horses were "roughed" to be able to get to the meet i.e. Shoes were roughened with a file to prevent the horse slipping

Scout lame in front and behind

Monday, March 18th

Chapel House. Rode Scout & Mr Pritchard's Gold Dust, Mabel Lancer & Lorna Doone.

Found in Salford Osiers, ran through Over Norton and killed in one of the Heythrop covers. Gorse between Salford and Cornwell blank. Found on Adlestrop Hill, ran below Chastleton Hill and turned right-handed over the hill, right-handed again, nearly to the bottom of the Adlestrop Hill road, turned left up into Daylesford and finally lost. Found in the Harcombs, ran a little circle in the vale and back to the Harcombs, out at the bottom again, and whipped off a vixen in Chastleton Grove. Scout was going a little lame in front and behind, and I lamed Gold Dust in the afternoon and went home miserable. There was a horribly strong north-west wind which I think prevented the foxes from getting away in to the vale. There was quite a nice scent when they did get there.

I lamed Gold Dust in the afternoon

Tuesday, March 19th

Barton House. Warwickshire. Rode Warrior.

Barton Grove blank; found in Wolford Wood and after running about a bit got away to Evenlode Mains where we lost. Found in Aston Hailes, ran through Dunsdon to Wolford Wood where we lost. Drew some more of Wolford Wood and I came home. Cold, and a very strong wind.

Friday, March 22nd.

Merrymouth. Rode the Nun, Mabel Lorna Doone, Sophie Bogy.

Found in Taynton Quarries, ran a few fields and lost. Tangley blank. Barrington covers blank. Fox viewed near Great Rissington, but the hounds hardly owned to it and soon gave up. Rissington Common and spinnies by the river blank. Got on the line of a fox between Wyck and Little Rissington, ran nicely to below Little Rissington and lost.

Home miserable

Found in far Gawcomb cover and came away at the bottom, turned left-handed across the Gawcomb ditch, up the hill past Icomb and lost by Maugersbury Grove. A warm, rather slack day. No scent on the hill, but seemed to be quite a nice one in the vale.

(She now appears to go to stay with Bijou Arkwright).

Tuesday, March 26th

Ryton. North Warwickshire. Rode Warrior.

Found Ryton Coppice, ran through Wappenbury and lost near Eathorpe. Eathorpe spinnies blank. Found in Frankton, ran to ground just outside. Found in Princethorpe, ran through Duke's Wood, Wappenbury and left-handed on to the hare farm, and back, losing in Princethorpe. Bull and Butcher and Reyton Wood blank. Hot and not much scent.

"No scent on the hill"

Wednesday, March 27th

The Balsall Windmill, North Warwickshire. Rode Scout.

Found in Rough Close and lost near Buckswell. Drew all their covers blank; Millicent, etc. blank. Found Tile Hill, ran through North Waste and back towards Buckswell. Plant's Hill, Park Wood, Top Wood, Black Waste and Long Meadow blank. Ground getting very hard. A terribly hot day.

"Quite a nice scent
in the Vale"

Saturday, March 30th

Bird-in-Hand, North Warwickshire. Rode Warrior.

Arrived late having missed the way and lost a good gallop from Mockley. Found Skilts Gorse, ran round the house on the left through Poole's Wood and lost in Barrels Park; they ran very fast. Hounds divided near Skilts and went off in 3 lots. All the Umberslade covers blank. Very hot and still no signs of rain. Scent good.

Gawcomb Ditch

Monday, April 1st

Chipping Norton Junction. Rode Stokey's hireling *(Mr Stokey kept a yard at Bourton Station)*, Mabel Lancer & Lorna Doone, Sophie Bogy, Mother Spider.

Spent the whole day in Bruern and Bould Wood and killed two foxes, the latter getting away as far as Idbury, where they killed and went home as the hounds had had enough, as the weather was boiling hot. They went home at 4.30 pm.

---

46 DAYS REGULAR HUNTING — 12 DAYS CUBBING.
WARRIOR 21 DAYS REGULAR HUNTING;
SCOUT 17 DAYS REGULAR HUNTING.

APRIL MAY 1905/1906

Potato Planting

ROCKLIFFE: DOWER HOUSE OF EYFORD

SEASON 1907-1908

Friday, Sep. 27th

Crawthornes, 6 o'clock. Rode Scout, Mabel Lancer.

Found and killed in Crawthornes before we got there. Found in Crabbie; ran to ground between Donnington and Banks Fee. Found in Banks Fee privet cover and also on Mary's Mound. Scout disgustingly fresh and did his best to buck me off. Scent fairly good.

Wednesday, Oct. 2nd

Oddington Ashes, 6.30. Rode Warrior, Mabel Lorna Doone.

Found and killed in Oddington Ashes. Found and killed in Baywell (a Daylesford cover). Found in Adlestrop Station Osier Bed, ran to Adlestrop village and lost. Found a lot of foxes in Mrs Thursby's cover and killed 2. A very pleasant morning with a fair scent.

Friday, Oct. 4th

Sezincote, 6.30. Rode Scout, Mabel Lancer.

Found and finally killed a Sezincote fox. Scout not so objectionally fresh. Scent bad.

Lots of foxes come out of Beans

Saturday, Oct. 5th

Worton Heath, 6.30. Stayed at Over Norton and rode Rex. Rosie *(Daly)* rode Pioneer, Captain Daly Parnell & Ravenbury.

Found and lost in Worton Heath. Drew a good many small covers blank. Found and chopped 2 foxes in turnip fields near Tracey's Farm and after a fast little circle lost in Tracey's Farm — several foxes came out of the same patch of beans which was being cut.

Friday, Oct. 11th

Cold Aston. Rode Scout & Warrior, Mabel Lorna Doone.

Drew some covers out towards Notgrove blank. Found in Aston Grove, ran round about a bit and finally killed near the Grove. Drew outlying covers on the borders of the Cotswold blank. Found a lot of foxes in Redesdale's Gorse, ran 3 to ground in the Gorse, went away with another and lost above Slaughter. Ground getting a little softer.

Wednesday, Oct. 16th

Gawcomb. Rode Warrior, Mabel Lorna Doone.

Found plenty of foxes in Gawcomb; finally killed one. Drew Wyck Hill Kennel Copse blank.

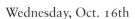

Found in Botany Bay, ran through Maugersbury Grove and killed him in a ditch just below. I then went home as I had to catch the 12.20 train to London. They found in Oddington Upper Ashes, had a very good run and killed near Idbury. Only Sturman, Will and Mr Barnsley saw anything of it. Ground quite soft enough, after days of pouring rain. Good scent.

Friday, Oct. 18th

Bourton Wood. Rode Scout, Mabel Lancer, Mother Bogy.

A very great many foxes in Bourton Wood, one of which they killed. Batsford blank. Found below Cadley Arbour, ran round about Aston Magna and killed close to where found. A pouring wet morning and we were soaked to the skin. Medium scent.

Monday, Oct. 21st

Tangley. Rode Warrior, Mabel Lorna Doone, Mother Bogy.

A great many foxes in Tangley but they did not manage to kill one. Taynton Quarries blank. Went away from Tangley towards Great Rissington but hounds could make very little of it. Scent not bad in cover first thing. A most glorious sunny autumn morning.

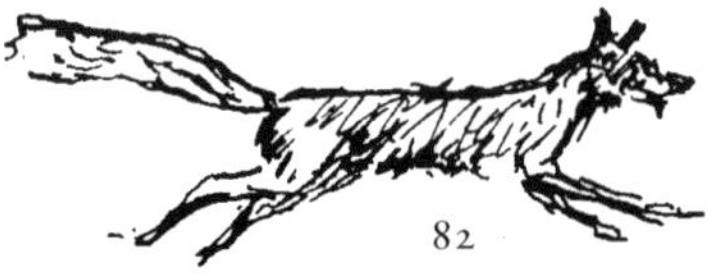

"A nice lot of little walls to jump"

Friday, Oct. 25th

Farmington Grove. Rode Warrior, Mabel Lancer, Mother Bogy.

Arrived rather late. They had, I think, found in the Grove and gone out as far as Farmington Lodge. Drew the Firs blank. Found in Long Plantation (my own name) and dragged on finally to Lodge Park. Found the same or another fox, then ran a little way out and back again. We came home. Quite a cheerful morning with a lot of little walls to jump. Shall be very glad when Warrior's new saddle comes as I nearly fall off this one over the jumps. Wet morning and got wet through.

Saturday, Oct. 26th

Kineton Thorns. N. Cotswold. Rode Scout, Mabel Lorna Doone.

Found in Lee Wood but soon lost. Found in Kineton Thorns, ran through Lee and Lark Wood back to Kineton Thorns, out of Kineton Thorns the Eyford end, by Guiting Park, Guiting Brake and lost near Tally Ho Quarries. I saw nothing of the hounds after Kineton Thorns the second time, as I got left there with nearly the whole field, the Master, first whip and about 3 couple of hounds. Mabel got away with them — I feel disgusted! Foggy first thing, cleared later. Scent must have been good in the open.

This appears to be Frances, second from the left, and Mabel in the centre of the photograph.

A local country house, possibly Sarsden.

Mabel and Jack Cheetham.

Iaking a short rest.

Eileen (age 9) Denise (age 5) Lilah (aged 1)

Monday, Oct. 28th

Chapel House. Rode Warrior.

Found in a root field near Rollright; ran through Rollright village, turned back left-handed and down the bottom a little way, then turned right-handed over the hill and to ground in Barton Grove. A very slow hunt; scent bad. Drew Salford Osiers; found, ran slowly up over the hill close to Cross Hands, turned to the left over Adlestrop Hill and lost in Daylesford Park.

Eileen, Denise and Lilah Daly *(aged 9, 5 and 1)* were all riding after the hounds so were Tony Moon aged 8 *(from Heythrop Rectory)* and a little Hall boy. They have killed 21½ brace in 23 days.

Mabel got away with them

Thursday, Oct. 31st

Guy's Cliffe. North Warwickshire. Rode Bijou's Clumber.

Found in a turnip field, ran across our field and killed on river bank. Drew several root fields and small covers. Found at Guy's Cliffe, ran across a field and had to whip off in the streets of Warwick. Found in cover where Piers Galveston was beheaded, ran a circle and back through the same cover and to ground a few fields on. Quite nice and exciting. Clumber does jump and gallop beautifully. Enjoyed my mount most awfully. Not more than 12 people out. We had to go over the most awful wooden bridge. Clumber behaved perfectly, but almost everyone else led over. Scent medium.

"I feel disgusted"

"Mr. Pritchard made his first appearance in red coat which becomes him."

Monday, Nov. 4th

Heythrop. Rode Scout, Mabel Lancer. Mabel and I stayed at Heythrop.

Found in the Ovens, ran towards Banbury Lodge, turned short right-handed and lost near Heythrop church. Found 3 foxes in cover near the Kennels; after some time one got away towards Tew, but soon lost. Drew one or two covers near Tew blank. Came back to Heythrop and found close to the House; ran him about for some time and then gave it up. A typical opening meet day and a very bad scent.

Warrior fit and well

Wednesday, Nov. 6th

Bradwell Grove. Rode Warrior, Mabel Lorna Doone.

Stayed at Over Norton the night before and was motored to Burford. Mabel motored with the Pritchards. Mr Pritchard made his first appearance in his red coat, which becomes him. Found in Bradwell Grove, ran a little way out the other side and lost. Found in cover just this side of Bradwell Grove, ran by Westwell, through Westwell Poor Lots, nearly to Barrington, turned right-handed towards Burford, checked for a little, then ran back again into Bradwell Grove and finally killed. A very nice gallop; about 35 minutes without a check and altogether a good deal over an hour. Warrior very fit and well.

Mabel motored with Pritchards (to the meet)

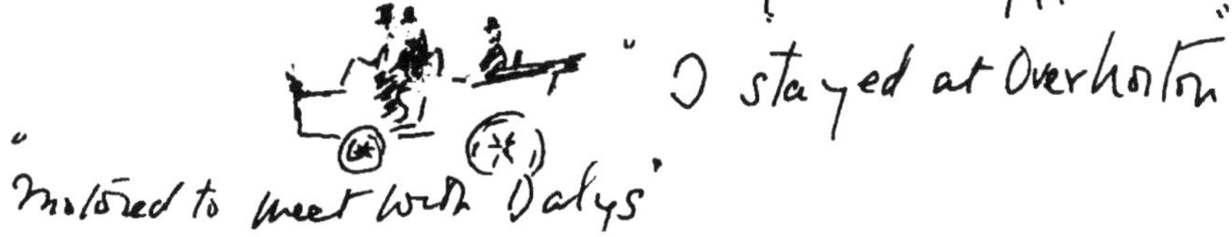

"I stayed at Overnorton"
"motored to meet with Dalys"

Friday, Nov. 8th

Stow-on-the-Wold. Rode Scout, Mabel Lancer, Mother Spider.

A foggy morning. Slaughter Copses blank. Found at Copse Hill, ran out a little way towards Eyford, turned back past Copse Hill again, across the brook between Upper and Lower Slaughter and up onto the hill and lost. The new larch plantation blank. Found close to Swiss Cottage, but lost almost at once. Found at Eyford; ran out towards the slate quarries, checked and the hounds were taken home on account of the fog. A wretched day; the scent very bad.

Monday, Nov. 11th

Ledwell Village. Rode Warrior, Mabel Lorna Doone.

Horses were sent on to Heythrop the night before. Found in Worton Heath and, after some time in the cover, ran fast for the first few fields and then slowly with a good many checks to North Aston and on to Middle Aston, and finally lost. Drew some of the Barton covers blank. Found in Seagrave's Osiers; ran nearly to Worton Heath, turned short right-handed, through Duns Tew then rather to the left, in the direction of Deddington; then right-handed again, over Dean Hill and killed close to North Aston House. A good run and very fast, quite as much as our horses could manage. We had about 20 miles to ride back and got home about 6 o'clock, having thoroughly enjoyed our day. Warrior is wonderfully fit and well.

Crossing The Adlestrop Railway Bridge
(No Bridge between there + Evenlode)

Wednesday, Nov. 13th

Chipping Norton Junction. Rode Scout, Mabel Lancer.

Icomb Cow Pastures blank, also Icomb Place. Found in Gawcomb; ran into the far cover, then back again and out the Wyck Hill end, turned sharp ran very nicely a good deal more than half way to Tangley and then back again to Gawcomb when I came home. They ran out towards Tangley again and killed their fox. Scout seemed to get done rather easily.

Friday, Nov. 15th

Moreton. Mabel rode Lorna Doone.

A very good run.

Scout sprang a curb

Saturday, Nov. 16th

Shipton-under-Wychwood. Rode Warrior.

Found in Shipton Court gardens and ran to ground in a wood pile. A couple of hounds and a terrier were left behind to get him out and they killed him. Found and killed at once in a small osier bed in Shipton. Chopped a fox in Shipton Barrow. Found in Widley, ran through Hensgrove and after a nice gallop killed in a cover above Ascott. Found a lame fox close by and killed him. Drew Hensgrove blank. Halloaed on to a fox which ran through Hensgrove and was lost. Killed 2½ brace.

Sowing from bucket hung from hook, suspended from neck.

Monday, Nov. 18th

Chapel House. Rode Scout, Mabel Lancer, whom she took home soon as he was not going very sound as he sprung a curb not long ago.

Found in Walk Gorse; ran a few fields towards Salford Osiers, ran through the osiers, up over the hill near Rollright Stones and to ground by the road on the hill going down into Long Compton. Found on Adlestrop Hill, ran round about for some time but finally got away towards the Harcombs which we left on our right; ran down into the vale to the left of Evenlode, across the Evenlode — Adlestrop road, up to the brook, which the hounds crossed and we could not, so went round by Adlestrop station and got to the hounds again in Mrs Thursby's covers where they lost. A good gallop, and Scout went well, though he needed a lot of sending along. Several falls in blind ditches. Scout was very stiff indeed behind next day, and Mr Renfrew thinks very badly of him. He says it is something of the nature of paralysis and will get worse.

Mangol Pulling

Friday, Nov. 22nd

New Barn. Rode Warrior, Mabel Lorna Doone.

Found in Lodge Park and killed him; went away on another, ran out somewhere near Notgrove, then right-handed through Aston Grove into Cold Aston village where they thought they had got him in a garden and spent a long time looking for him amongst ivy, etc. without success. However, he jumped up in a hedgerow just outside the village, ran through Aston Grove, by Farmington Pillars, skirted Farmington Grove, and killed him in a Sherborne cover alongside the Burford — New Barn road. Another fox went away while they were eating the last, but though the hounds started well, the fox twisted about and finally was lost. The first run was very good. There were a good many VWH and Cotswold people out.

Monday, Nov. 25th

Pomfret Castle. Rode Scout, who went rather stiff when he began cantering.

Found in Badger's Gorse; ran two circles round by Swerford Park and back again to Badger's Gorse and finally killed just outside Swerford Park. Drew Tew Pond Tail, Cow Hill, French's Hollow and some little hanging covers close by blank. I then came home as they were still drawing away from home.

Sheep dipping

Wednesday, Nov. 27th

Stow Station. Rode Warrior, Mabel Lorna Doone.

Stow Bridge copse blank. Found in little cover on side of the hill just this side of Little Rissington; ran out at top, then turned left-handed, ran down through Wyck Rissington and across the vale to Bourton; then turned left-handed nearly to Rissington Common and then up over the hill and left-handed back past the cover where we found; down through Wyck Rissington and into the vale again where they lost him, but he was viewed, run to ground and killed near Bourton. Drew Kennel Copse and Botany Bay blank. Fox was viewed just going into Maugersbury Grove, but there did not seem much scent and we soon lost. Drew Icomb cover blank. Found in Gawcomb, ran out at the top across the road, turned left-handed and crossed the Stow road, nearly to Maugersbury and lost. The first part of the run in the morning was nice.

'Bagging hook' which was superseded by the scythe

Friday, Nov. 29th

Moreton. Rode Scout, who was rather stiff.

Found in Crawthornes, ran out to the larch cover close by, was headed back into Crawthornes again, ran out towards Frogmoor and lost. Found in Crabby, ran nearly to Broadwell church, turned right, ran through the Fish Pond coppice, then left-handed up over Tump Ground, crossed the Stow road, left Donnington Brewery on the left, past Mrs Godman's Windmill nearly to Condicote; after which scent failed and they dragged on to Hensgrove and lost.

DONNINGTON BREWERY

Drew Dibden's Gorse blank. Fox was halloaed in the direction of the Beehive Lodges and they ran across the Stow — Evesham road and Sezincote lane and to ground in a bank just this side of Bourton-on-the-Hill. Found near Sezincote House; ran a small circle in the vale, then up over the hill near Bourton Quarries, through the bottom of Bourton Wood, across Dovedale and over the Stow — Broadway road to Springhill, when I came home. They went on for about 3 miles and then gave up. Scout was hardly able to move next morning.

Monday, Dec. 2nd

Boulter's Barn. Rode Warrior, Mabel Lorna Doone.

Found in Sarsgrove; ran all round about it for a long time and lost. Found in the Partridge cover; ran, some of the time rather nicely, to Chapel House and lost. Found in the Norrels, ran up past Sarsden Pillars and over the Chipping Norton — Shipton road, turned right-handed down alongside the road, then recrossed it, where scent suddenly failed. We dragged on up to the Jubilee Plantation and then went home. Poor day.

Friday, Dec. 6th

Barrington New Inn. Rode Warrior, Mabel Lorna Doone.

Several covers including Windrush Poor Lots blank. Found in gorse not far from Bradwell Grove but soon lost. Patcat gorse blank. Found close by; ran out towards Williamstrip to Lakenwell where we came home. A very nice gallop. Scent very bad in the morning as it was sticky after a frost, but improved very much later.

Wednesday, Dec. 11th

Adlestrop. Rode Warrior, Mabel Lorna Doone.

Found in osiers by Adlestrop station, ran very fast to the Harcombs, then fox stayed there a little time, but finally went away up over the hill nearly to Adlestrop village, then doubled back and went into some farm buildings in Chastleton where he was killed. Next we drew Oddington Ashes; found, ran a small circle out towards the Spotted Pig, twisted about the village and Ashes for some time, but at last went away and ran without a check by Mrs Thursby's covers to Crawthornes, right through and out the other side for a few fields, then back into Crawthornes and out again through Frogmoor, across the Evenlode to Evenlode Mains, tried to get back to Crawthornes, but they killed him just the Evenlode side of the railway. A very good run indeed. I did not see any more after they crossed the Evenlode, as I tried to jump it and got in, and had very great difficulty in getting Warrior out. Fortunately he was none the worse. It was my fault that he got in. The country is most frightfully wet and deep.

Monday, Dec. 16th

Chapel House. Rode Warrior, Mabel Lorna Doone.

Found in Walk Gorse, ran out towards the railway and Badger's Gorse but soon lost. Drew Choice Hill Osiers and a few other little covers blank. Found in Salford Osiers; ran up the hill towards the Stow — Banbury road, but either he was a very twisty fox or he was continually headed, for he never ran straight for more than a field or two, so though the hounds hunted him well for some time, they lost him near Cornwell. Found on Adlestrop Hill but again fox would not go straight and we went backwards and forwards over Chastleton Hill and Adlestrop Hill. They did at last go away through Little Compton where we left them casting in the direction of Barton Grove. A very disappointing day and tiring for the horses.

Friday, Dec. 20th

Stow-on-the-Wold. Rode Col. Meyrick's horse Kruger with the idea of buying him; *(Colonel Meyrick came from Chastleton Glebe and at one point rented Fosse Cottage)*, Mabel Lorna Doone.

Found in one of Mr Fenwick's new covers on the hill above Swell.

"Bowes Daly was out looking very smart in new riding kit"

Ran past Abbotswood stables, crossed the Stow — Nether Swell road (i.e. Lower Swell), up the hill and through allotments above Quar Wood, through Maugersbury Park, and killed in one of the yards at the back of Park Street in Stow. The fox ran right through Mr Robert Blizard's kitchen and rather interfered with preparations for dinner! Found in cover near Swell Wold, ran round about the Eyford covers for some time, then got away to Kineton Thorns, and then on again to Guiting Quarries and killed near Trafalgar. I liked Colonel Meyrick's yellow horse Kruger and if he passes the vet we are going to buy him for £125. Scout is quite sound again but we are afraid to try to hunt him for fear his back should go again.

Monday, Dec. 23rd

Pomfret Castle. Rode Warrior, Mabel was mounted by the Moons.

Found in Badgers Gorse; ran round by Swerford and back to Badgers Gorse; out again past Pomfret Castle, through Tew Pond Tail, right-handed up the hill, crossed the road between Great Tew and Little Tew, left Tracey's farm on our left, turned right-handed down the Green Lane and lost in Heythrop, when I came home. Hounds fortunately did not run very fast, as the going was too awful. It was quite a nice run though, only spoilt by the heavy going. Bowes Daly *(aged 7)* was out looking very smart in new riding kit on the new grey pony.

Friday, Dec. 27th

Merrymouth. Rode Warrior, Mabel Lorna Doone, Sophie Kruger.

Found in Tangley and after running round for some time came out at this end and went right-handed over the hill and down past Westcote into the Gawcomb vale; turning left-handed they left Icomb Cow Pastures about two fields on their right, through the lower end of the Upper Ashes, across the line and to Marjorie Copse, where they checked for a little; then right-handed over the hill to Caudle Copse, then left-handed up the ravine and killed in the open about a field below the Stow allotments.

They make it a 7-mile point, but I should hardly have thought it as much. The part in the Gawcomb vale was ripping and Warrior was an angel. A good many people were left behind in Tangley and others at the Gawcomb ditch. On their way back to draw the Barrington covers a fox jumped up by the roadside in Barrington Lane and they killed him in a little hanging cover above Wyck Rissington. Found in Rissington Common; ran, not very straight, but some of the time fast, across the hill into Gawcomb and out a few fields into the vale at the bottom and lost. It was a bitterly cold day and the scent, specially in the morning, was good. It was inclined to freeze all day. I rode Warrior with a spur so as to send him a bit faster at his fences sometimes. He had got into rather a bad habit of refusing to go out of a trot and the spur had an excellent effect. I hope I shan't need it again.

(A hard frost and one day's skating).

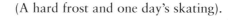

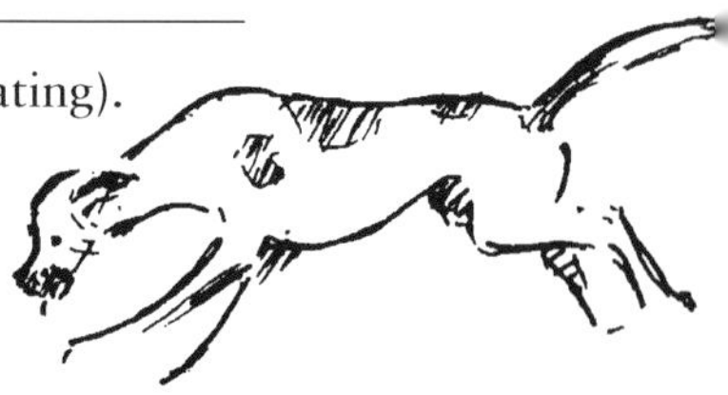

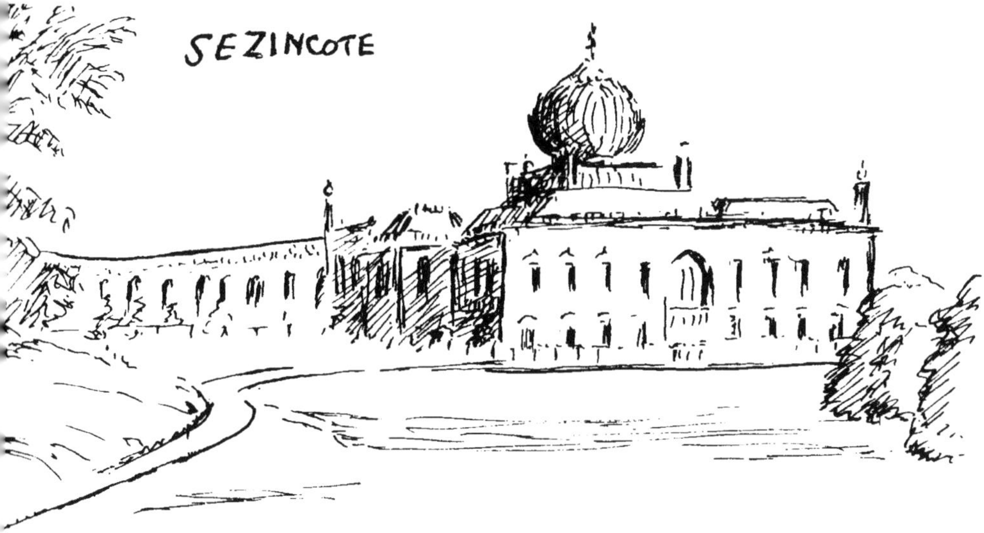
SEZINCOTE

Wednesday, Jan. 8th

Bledington Mill. Rode Warrior, Mabel Lorna Doone.

Fox running up
across in front
of Sezincote

Found and ran round about in Bould Wood for a long time, but at last got away and ran very nicely to Tangley where they lost. The whole field, except Captain Daly, Sturman, and Will and myself were left in Bould Wood. Found in Bruern and spent the rest of the day between there and Bould Wood. The frost was fairly out of the ground but it was frightfully rotten. (Another frost has set in and it looks like it's lasting.)

Friday, Jan. 17th

Moreton. Rode Kruger & Warrior, Mabel Lancer & Lorna Doone.

Rook Hill blank. Found in gorse by Cadley Arbour, also chopped a fox there; ran into Bourton Wood and about there for some time; fox broke away in the direction of Blockley station, but was headed back into the wood and after some time got away to Batsford; ran down through the gardens and into the vale as far as the Moreton — Longborough road where they checked; then right-handed through Thickleather and Blackthorns, past Sezincote House, across Sezincote lane and finally killed after doubling backwards and forwards a bit.

Mabel tries new horse

Went back to Bourton Wood where there were a lot of foxes about. Spent a long time there, and then went and drew the covers below Cadley Arbour, but they were blank and hounds went home. I was very pleased with the way Kruger went in the vale below Batsford as we had some big things to jump. The ground was very rotten after the frost.

which has been bought. Big long-tailed horse up to unnecessary weight

Monday, Jan. 20th

Chapel House. Rode Warrior & Kruger, Mabel Lorna Doone & Lancer.

Found in Walk Gorse; ran into Over Norton Park and lost. Gorse above Salford Osiers blank. Found in Salford Osiers; ran fast to the Rollright — Chapel House road where they checked, then on through Walk Gorse to Badgers Gorse, where they took on a fresh fox which they ran to Heythrop. After galloping about Heythrop for some time we came home. It was most disappointing that the hounds did not get to Adlestrop Hill as we had second horses waiting there. I fell off Kruger in Over Norton Park. I was talking to Bijou, who was driving, when Kruger suddenly shied away and I toppled off! Captain Daly lost White Socks, who broke his back jumping a small fence soon after the hounds left Salford.

Wednesday, Jan. 22nd

Adderbury. Rode De Wet, Mabel Pioneer. Stayed at Over Norton.

Drew small covers near Adderbury blank. Found in new gorse cover close to Wilson's Gorse; ran through Wilson's Gorse and very fast for a bit till they got onto the hill country where they did not run so well. I do not know where we went but we finally lost in Adderhury.

Zara Pollock very pleasant & conversational

Kruger in Temper

Found at
Dean Hill. Started away well but soon lost. Found in Duns Tew Gorse ran across the river, but soon turned short back again across the river into Duns Tew Gorse again, then back again across the river and nearly to Deddington; then back again to Duns Tew Gorse, where they gave up and went home. They say 12 people got into the brook. And some people who got over the first time got in the second, as did Zara Pollock. Sturman got in the first time. Neither Mabel nor I got over nor in!

Shamrock contrary

Friday, Jan. 24th

New Barn. Rode Warrior, Mabel Lorna Doone.

Found in Lodge Park ran to Farmington village where we lost. As we were going back to draw a thick fog came on and as it did not lift hounds went home.

Saturday, Jan. 25th

Trooper's Lodge. N. Cotswold. Rode Kruger, Mabel Lancer.

Scout Bucking

Found in gorse below Springhill Lower Lodge; ran into Springhill covers where we spent some time and finally lost. Found and ran across into Dovedale, up nearly to Trooper's Lodge, then right-handed alongside the Broadway road; then left-handed into Springhill where we stayed a little, then on to Middle Hill where we lost. Found in a tree at Middle Hill, ran fast to Buckland Wood, then back again to Middle Hill, where I left them. I don't know when I've been up and down so many banks. The hounds are so slow coming to Sir John Campbell.

Monday, Jan. 27th

Pomfret Castle. Rode Warrior, Mabel Lorna Doone.

Warrior pulling

Tew Pond Tail blank. Found in Tew Gardens; ran fast to Sandford where we checked, then on to Worton Heath; came out the far end, ran on very slowly by Nether Worton and lost by Duns Tew Gorse.

We had quite made up our minds that we were going to have the Deddington brook again, but we were spared that. Found on Dean Hill but there seemed very little scent and we finally lost close to Deddington. Found and chopped a fox below Hawk Hill. Iron Down, Falkland's Bushes, etc. blank. Found in Badgers Gorse after we had gone home. We did not get home till nearly 6 o'clock after a most unsatisfactory day.

Wednesday, Jan. 29th

Bradwell Grove. Rode Kruger, Mabel Lancer.

Found in Bradwell Grove, but as soon as we got out of the cover there was no scent and we soon lost. Drew several Bradwell Grove covers blank, found in one at last but soon lost. Found in gorse cover alongside the road near Patcat Gorse; ran a fairly fast circle getting within a few fields of Burford. We left them running slowly back towards Bradwell Grove, having presumably changed foxes, as, soon after we left the hounds, we came on a group of people on foot looking at a fox lying in a field close to the road and which they said was the hunted fox; they had seen it come up and lie down there — it never moved when a man walked up and stood right over it! But then a dog saw it, went and jumped on its back, rolled it over, when it jumped up, came over the wall into the road, down which it went a few yards and then turned into someone's garden and we saw it no more.

Friday, Jan. 31st

Moreton. Rode Mr Fenwick's Curate, Mabel Lorna Doone.

Found and chopped a fox in small cover in Moreton recreation ground, ran across the Moreton — Batsford road, turned right-handed and over the Worcester and the Shipston lines, right through Wolford Wood without a pause, through Dunsdon, turned right-handed through Todenham, soon after which we changed foxes and lost by Lower Wolford. Will had seen a fox going into a barn near Todenham so we went back there and found him waiting for us and killed him. This was no doubt the hunted fox. We trotted back to Moreton, where we found a man with a fox in a bag which he had caught in a fowl house, where it had taken refuge when we were drawing the cover in Moreton recreation ground. He let the fox out just outside Moreton and we simply raced up to Batsford and then slowly on to Bourton Wood and lost. Found in the Banks Fee privet cover, ran up the hill in the direction of Stow, but soon turned left-handed down into the vale below Donnington and across it nearly to Sezincote Lower Lodge, then turned left-handed up the hill, right on to Sezincote Warren and out the other side, then back again and finally lost. I came home from below Sezincote as the Curate could go no farther. He is a splendid fencer, not in very good condition.

"They say 12 people got into the Brook some people got over Neither Mabel or I got over or in!"

A meet with traditional haystacks as a background.

John and Bobby Kennard.

Susan and Nancy Kennard with their aunt Mabel.

The road from Lower Swell.

Monday, Feb. 3rd

Boulter's Barn. Rode Warrior, Mabel Lancer.

A typical Boulter's Barn day. We found in Sarsgrove, ran round about but did not get far away and finally lost. Found in the Partridge cover, ran towards Sarsgrove, then down into the Norrels, back again towards Sarsden and lost. Drew the Norrels blank. Found in Churchill Heath, ran fast across to Bould Wood, and the hunted fox went straight through, but hounds changed and we spent ages galloping about the wood and at last gave it up. We went back to Churchill Heath and again found, ran nearly to the Norrels and lost, and hounds went home. I think scent was fairly good but things went contrary.

Friday, Feb. 7th

Farmington Grove. Rode Warrior, Mabel Lorna Doone.

Found in the Firs, ran into Farmington Grove, ran about there for a bit, then out to Sherborne where we hung about for some time, but finally got away across the New Barn — Burford road, but it was a bad twisting fox and the hounds were hardly able to run at all and finally we lost altogether. Some of the Sherborne covers, the osier beds by the river, and Sherborne Cow Pastures blank, also Clapton Gorse; we found in a small cover near Clapton Gorse and ran very fast up over the hill to Farmington Grove where they turned back sharp left-handed and out towards Sherborne but killed just before they got there. 23 minutes and very nice.

Saturday, Feb. 8th

Sezincote Warren. Rode Kruger, but came home early as he did not seem well. Mabel rode Lancer.

It was not much of a day.

Wednesday, Feb. 12th

Adlestrop. Rode Warrior, Mabel Lorna Doone.

Osier bed by Adlestrop station blank. Found in Oddington Ashes, and the main body of the pack went away towards the Upper Ashes, while Sturman and a few hounds and the field remained in the Ashes. We came upon the hounds by the railway and in the Upper Ashes, and from there ran along the line to below Maugersbury, then turned right-handed up the hill by Mr Evans's house, then right-handed down the hill again and killed close to the shooting butts. Captain Daly cricked his back jumping a ditch below Maugersbury and had to go home. Drew Marjorie Copse where there were two foxes. We ran by the Spotted Pig, through Upper Oddington to Mrs Thursby's covers, then on up the ravine to the highest Caudle Copse where they turned left-handed and across the Stow — Oddington road and killed in Maugersbury Park. Drew Mrs Thursby's cover blank. Found in Oddington Upper Ashes, ran to Maugersbury Grove and back to the Upper Ashes and lost. Icomb Cow Pastures blank. Cover by Icomb blank. Found in Gawcomb and got away at the bottom, a long way behind our fox, ran slowly, with many checks, a circle in the Gawcomb vale and came up over the hill near Icomb and into Wyck Hill covers. A fox went away at the bottom and we ran him as far as the Bourton — Stow road and lost. Rather a nice cheerful day, but very hot.

Muck Spreading. There was 9 yards between heaps and between rows of heaps of manure.

Friday, Feb. 14th

Merrymouth. Rode Kruger, Mabel Lancer.

Jogged all round by Barrington and drew everything blank till we got back to Tangley about 1 o'clock, where we found at once and ran out near the Merrymouth as if for Bould Wood; but turned sharp right-handed in to Milton and then on by Shipton station and back into Bruern. After they got into Milton it was very slow and hounds did not actually take a line into Bruern.

Fox went away from Bruern into Bould Wood, where we galloped round a bit and hounds finally slipped away out by Foscote, ran fast to Gawcomb; Sturman, Will, Mabel, Mr and Mrs Moon and Mr Parker, being the only ones with them. I caught them at Gawcomb and they ran out at the bottom by Icomb village and then right-handed into the vale and killed within a field of Bould Wood. A very good run. Only Sturman and Will saw the whole of it. Zara, Colonel Meyrick, Mr Harding, Mr Evered and I saw the end. Kruger went well, but had had about enough. Neither Mr Brassey nor Captain Daly were out. Captain Daly is laid up with acute rheumatism as a result of his crick in the back of Wednesday.

Monday, Feb. 17th

Chapel House. Rode Warrior, Mabel Lorna Doone.

Found in Walk Gorse; ran out at the bottom, then turned right-handed and ran very fast to Heythrop; ran about there for a long time and finally killed him in the Ovens. It was rather nice as there was such a good scent. Found in Salford Osiers; ran up the hill across the Rollright road, down to Barton Grove from where we took, I think, a fresh fox on across the road just above Long Compton, and on through Rollright Combes into Wychford Wood; turned left-handed down the wood, and out; ran very fast a few fields back in the direction of Rollright and lost. Hounds went home. A good day and a very good scent. I had hounds to myself for about 3 fields! ! ! ! and nearly found myself in the bottom of a large ditch as a result! !

Wednesday, Feb. 19th

North Aston. Stayed at Heythrop. Rode Kruger, Mabel Lancer.

Found in osier bed below North Aston ran round about North Aston House, then to Dean Hill where there was more than one fox. We came away after one that took us by Duns Tew village to Worton Heath, where I think we changed, and a few hounds went on to Barton, where after a short time Sturman followed with the rest of the pack; from Barton we did a circle round by Middle Aston and Steeple Aston back to Barton and then out again to Steeple Aston where we killed. A good run, though after Worton Heath the country was not good. We did not do any more as we had been galloping pretty well over two hours.

Friday, Feb. 21st

Moreton. Rode Warrior, Mabel Lorna Doone.

Found in Crawthornes ran fast to Banks Fee, then hunted on slowly through Sezincote Warren out to the Hornsleasow covers and back again towards Sezincote Warren and lost. Drew Dibden's Gorse, Hensgrove and covers up to Sezincote House blank. Found close to Sezincote House, ran up the hill, turned right-handed into Bourton Wood, out by Batsford, back again into Bourton Wood, then out again and killed in Bourton-on-the-Hill.

Got on the line of a fox near Sezincote Lower Lodge; ran very nicely but not very fast nearly to Little Barrow where they gave up. Scent was very good in the vale. The last little run was very nice and cheered one up after an otherwise rather annoying day. Captain Daly's back seemed about well again.

Monday, Feb. 24th

Pomfret Castle. Rode Kruger, Mabel Lancer.

Tew Pond Tail, and Tew Gardens blank. Chopped a fox in Sandford Park. Found in Worton Heath; ran a very fast little ten minutes to just below Over Worton and lost. Cast back to Worton Heath without success. Hawk Hill and Iron Down blank. Found and killed on Down Hill. Found another there, ran round about a bit and lost. French's Hollow, Swerford, and Badgers Gorse blank. Hounds went home. Mr Brassey had a strain and not allowed to hunt.

"Warrior down in a ditch"

Wednesday, Feb. 26th

Adlestrop. Rode Warrior, Mabel Lorna Doone.

Found on Adlestrop Hill; ran through the Harcombs very fast across the vale to Barton Grove, then hunted on up to the Rollright road, turned left-handed down the hill, then up through Rollright Combes into Whichford Wood where they marked him to ground. The first part to Barton Grove was splendid. I did not see anything after Rollright Combes as Warrior jumped short at a biggish ditch and hedge below Rollright Combes; we did not part company but got out on the wrong side; tried again, and again got in! Found in Evenlode Mains ran a circle back to Evenlode Mains. We then came home.

Muddy Back

Friday, Feb. 28th

Bourton-on-the-Water. Rode Kruger, Mabel Lancer.

Chopped a fox in Redesdale's Gorse. Fox halloaed by the railway; hounds ran a few fields and lost.

Kruger in Temper

All the boundary covers and Aston Grove blank. Found near Gilbert's Grave; ran below Farmington Grove out towards New Barn and lost. Found in little cover below Farmington Grove by the water, ran into Farmington Grove and back to ground in cover where they found.

Monday, March 2nd

Boulter's Barn. Rode Warrior, Mabel Lorna Doone.

Sarsgrove, Partridge Cover, Jubilee Plantation, etc. blank. Found in the Norrels; ran out a few fields and lost. Found in Churchill Heath, ran fairly straight to Pudlicote and killed. Found in Bruern, ran through Bould Wood, up the hill by Idbury, turned right-handed along the hill to Gawcomb; scent failed and hounds went home.

Scout Bucking

Tuesday, March 3rd

Ledwell Village. Rode Kruger, Mabel Lancer. Stayed at Ranger's Lodge Monday night and Over Norton Tuesday night with our horses.

It had snowed a good deal in the night and there was a good deal of snow at Ledwell village; hounds trotted straight off to North Aston to draw. They found in the spinnies down by the river ran to Dean Hill where several foxes went away. They finally got away after one which went across the river and up through Deddington; but they got farther and farther behind their fox and finally gave it up. It was rather a good hound run as they went very fast some of the time, but it was nearly impossible to keep actually with them. Found in osier bed near Adderbury, ran by Adderbury and left-handed very fast indeed down to an unjumpable brook which the hounds crossed and we could not, so had to go right-handed through Adderbury and came upon the hounds having checked by a ditch. Will halloaed the fox on, and they ran very nicely for some time and killed in a ditch below Barford. A good day.

Warrior pulling

Shamrock contrary

Saturday, March 7th

Trooper's Lodge. N. Cotswold. Rode Warrior, Mabel Lancer.

A very bad day; bad scent and country seemed short of foxes. There was one in Sedgecomb and also in Stayt's gorse. Warrior sprained his suspensory, and so has finished his season. It is very sad.

Friday, March 13th

Merrymouth. Rode Col. Meyrick's Stockings, Mabel Lancer.

Found in cover just below Merrymouth and ran into Tangley, then left-handed over the Burford road and down into Fifield Heath, then right-handed below Fifield, through Shipton Barrow to Taynton Quarries and Tangley and, after hunting him about for a long time, they killed him in the open about 3 fields from Taynton Quarries. I was some way behind the hounds from Fifield Heath to Shipton Barrow, and a great many people quite lost the hounds and did not appear for ages after, in Tangley. Made quite sure there was not a fox left in Tangley, and then went down to Bould Wood where they found and ran back to Tangley. Colonel Meyrick has lent me Stockings for the rest of the season as Kruger is laid up. I like him very much indeed, but he is only 5 this spring and rather small for me. Kruger is going very stiff from both his shoulders and has to have a rest.

Monday, March 16th

Chipping Norton. Rode Parnell and De Wet; stayed at Over Norton. Mabel Lorna Doone and Lancer.

Went straight to Salford Osiers, where they found, ran right-handed up the ditch, twisting about first one side then the other, then turned right-handed up the hill, through Over Norton Park and killed in a belt of trees on the far side. Found on Adlestrop Hill, ran 2 circles round the hill and Daylesford and killed in Baywell.

HORSES !!

Another fox halloaed up over the hill, ran left-handed down below Chastleton, then to the right across the vale to Little Compton where he was headed back up Chastleton Hill, and after running round about for some time, he got to ground in Chastleton village. They hunted him very well and it was hard luck not getting him. There was a very good scent. I liked Parnell very much indeed; it is a sad pity he has gone in the wind.

Friday, March 20th

Moreton-in-Marsh. Rode Stockings, Mabel Lancer.

Rook Hill blank. Found in Cadley Arbour, ran into Batsford, then into Bourton Wood and out the other side nearly as far as Churnell, then turned back into Norcomb Bottom, where they lost. Found in Bourton Wood, ran out past Trooper's Lodge, left-handed through Stayt's Gorse and into Sezincote Warren and hunted on slowly through Hensgrove and Dibden's Gorse, back through Hensgrove and up across the Broadway road and finally gave it up near Sezincote Lane. Stockings came home dreadfully lame behind and I was miserable, but it turned out that he had only hit himself and was quite sound next morning. Bourton Wood was boggier than I have ever known it.

Wednesday, March 25th

Chipping Norton. Rode Stockings, Mabel Lancer.

Found in Icomb Cow Pastures and went first towards Bledington then turned right-handed across the Gawcomb ditch; then the hounds must have turned right again, but we went straight on to Bould village, where a man told Sturman that he had seen them running back for Gawcomb, so we went along the road through Idbury, then over the hill and found the hounds the other side of the Burford road all by themselves; they went on nearly to Rissington Common, then turned right-handed and up through Little Rissington nearly to the Barrington lane, then right-handed towards Barrington, when I left them.

"Stockings came home dreadfully lame behind I was miserable."

Monday, March 30th

Boulter's Barn. Rode Stockings, Mabel Lancer.

Baddish day. Found in the Norrels and Churchill Heath. I came home when they went to Bruern, where they found and ran slowly to Ascott. A cart colt broke its neck stampeding over some rails, for which the owner claimed £35.

Thursday, April 2nd

Kingscote. Lord Fitzhardinge's *(Berkeley)*. Rode Mrs Scott's Royston and stayed at Lasborough. *(Mrs Scott was Lilian Brassey)*.

Not a very good day, but that was not expected as it was a hill meet. They killed a fox, and it was delightful riding about on a very nice mount. Most lovely views out over the Severn Vale.

Friday, April 3rd

New Barn. Rode Stockings, Mabel Lorna Doone.

Found and killed in Lodge Park. Found and ran a rather twisting run and lost near Coln St. Aldwyns. I came home from near Bibury as Stockings did not seem fit. It took me 3 hours and 20 minutes to get home.

Saturday, April 11th

Ascott. Rode Colonel Meyrick's Stockings and bay horse.

I found the hounds just after they had killed close to Ascott after a very short run. Drew the Forest for a very long time before we found and ran out a few fields towards Ascott, then back into the Forest to Ranger's Lodge, where after some time the hounds killed and broke up a badger! I left Stockings at Sandford Mount and was very sorry to say goodbye to him.

Monday, April 13th

Churchill, 8 o'clock. Rode Lorna Doone.

Drew the Norrels blank. Found in Churchill Heath and started in the direction of Bledington; then went back again and out towards Sarsden, but could not make anything of it. Found in Bruern, ran out nearly to Lyneham and lost. Went to a halloa near Fifield Heath, ran past Bould Village and about 4 fields towards Gawcombe, then sharp left-handed up the hill, then left-handed again below Idbury and Fifield to ground in Milton Quarries where they got him out and killed him. A very fast 25 minutes. I was hopelessly thrown out when they turned left-handed up the hill near the beginning. Sturman, Peggy, Jack Witts and Mr Railston were the only ones who really saw it. Peggy went very well indeed on Hilda's new horse.

Nearly swept over fall

Thursday, April 16th

Broadwell, 8 o'clock. Rode Lorna Doone.

Mrs Godman's Windmill cover, Banks Fee and Donnington blank! Found in Crawthornes and went to ground in larch cover close by. Crabby blank. Found in Oddington Ashes; ran out across the Evenlode and railway into Daylesford Park and gardens where we stayed a little, then on and killed just short of the Adlestrop Hill road. Owing to Mabel being at Bordighera I had these last two days on Lorna Doone, who was charming.

Tuesday, April 28th

Dartmoor Hounds. Rode very good hireling called 'Cornishman' staying at Sandwell, Harberton.

Found on the moor, ran through an appalling bog which brought a good many people down and terrified me absolutely, but thanks to my pony's cleverness I got safely out and caught up, the hounds having checked. They got on the line again and ran very fast to Piles Wood where they lost. A good run. The country to me is absolutely terrifying to ride over, it is so rough and rocky, over which one goes at a gallop and in continual fear of bogs. There are lots of rivers to cross, and one deep and very rocky rapid nearly swept me down over a fall. I almost thought that my last hour had come. We found again but did not do anything and Claudie and I went home. I enjoyed my day most enormously notwithstanding my moments of terror. The horse I rode must have been under 15 hands but a perfect darling.

SUMMER 1906
Harvesting with a horse-drawn Sailreaper to cut the corn.
The children made the bond, the women tied the sheaves, the men made the stooks.
Some farms had reapers and binders by 1906.

SWISS COTTAGE

CUB HUNTING SEASON 1908

Monday, Sep. 7th

Adlestrop Hill, 5.30. Rode Kruger, Mabel Lorna Doone.

Plenty of cubs both on the Hill and in the Harcombs. Killed about 6.

Friday, Sep. 11th

Foxholes. Rode Kruger.

Scent bad. Plenty of cubs but did not kill any.

Monday, Sep. 14th

Heythrop. Rode Rosie Daly's Kilkenny and stayed at Heythrop, to say goodbye to Zara before her departure for Australia.

Spent the whole morning round about the Kennel covers and killed 2 or 3 cubs. Liked Kilkenny.

Friday, Sep. 18th

Bourton Bridge. Rode Warrior, Mabel Lancer.

Found plenty of cubs in Redesdale's gorse and killed 3. Drew our gorse cover near Round Hill blank. Killed 2 cubs in one of the college covers. Warrior very fresh and hard to hold.

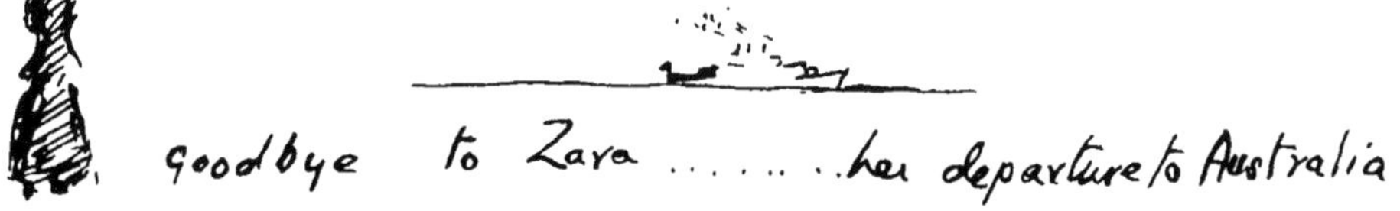
goodbye to Zara ....her departure to Australia

Thursday, Sep. 24th

Sezincote Warren. Rode Warrior, Mabel Lancer.

Spent the morning round about Sezincote Warren.

Friday, Sep. 25th

Batsford. Rode Kruger, Mabel Lorna Doone.

Found; ran to ground and killed in the Sally beds. Found above Batsford Gardens and marked to ground in a drain, which they dug out and killed 3. Did not go anywhere besides Batsford.

Wednesday, Sep. 30th

Eyford, 7.30. Rode Kruger, Mabel Lancer.

Hounds could not draw till about 8.30 on account of fog. There did not seem to be a great many foxes. Found one above Swiss Cottage, ran round by the slate quarries, through Eyford Park and killed on the road between Eyford and Brockhill Clump. Found again above Swiss Cottage and killed between there and Slaughter. A boiling hot morning. Kruger very fresh and pawed the air violently with his forelegs, to which I strongly object.

Left home soon after 7 o'clock

Thursday, Oct. 1st

Guiting Grange, 7.30. N. Cotswold. Rode Warrior.

Found 3 or 4 cubs in the top corner of Guiting Brake. One eventually got away, ran across the lawn of Guiting Grange, up the park and then left-handed to Lark and Lea Wood where they eventually killed. I felt frightfully thrilled at finding and having a run after one of our foxes! Another grilling hot day.

Friday, Oct. 2nd

Gawcomb, 7.30. Rode Kruger.

Could not put hounds in to draw till nearly 9 on account of thick fog. Found and spent a long time in Gawcomb but did not kill. The undergrowth is so very thick there early in the season. Found at Wyck Hill and also in the Icomb cover but did not kill. Weather hotter than ever. Kruger's behaviour excellent.

Monday, Oct. 5th

Oddington. Rode Warrior, Mabel Lancer.

Very foggy early, and stayed more or less so all the morning. Killed 3 cubs in osier bed by Adlestrop station, and at least 2 in withy bed below Cornwell. I was most extraordinarily lucky in finding my watch, which I discovered was missing out of my pocket when I started for home, and turned back and found it in the corner of a root field! Our last day from Fosse Cottage. Lorna Doone sprained her fetlock out at exercise and is I fear laid up for some time.

Long ride: home at 3 p.m.

"Most dreadfully hungry

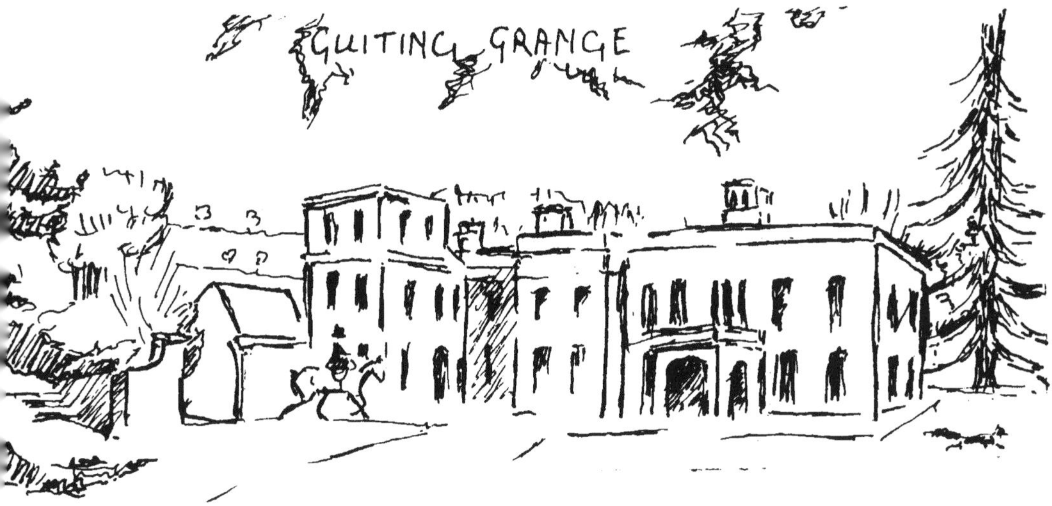

(From now on the family is living at Guiting Grange in the N. Cotswold country).

Monday, Oct. 12th

Foxholes, 8.30. Rode Kruger, Mabel Lancer.

Hounds gave a good many of us the slip in Bould Wood, ran across the vale and killed in Oddington Upper Ashes. The country was too blind for jumping. Found again in Bould Wood or Bruern, ran round about but did not kill while we were out. We found it a fearfully long ride to and from Guiting — we did not get back till nearly 3.00, most dreadfully hungry as we had had nothing since breakfast before 7.00.

Wednesday, Oct. 14th

Bradwell Grove. Rode Warrior.

Found hounds just as they killed a fox outside Bradwell Grove. Spent all the morning running round about the Grove. A most fearfully long ride from Guiting, about 15 miles.

Friday, Oct. 16th

Tangley. Rode Kruger, Mabel Lancer.

Spent all the morning running round about Tangley and Taynton Quarries. Weather still very hot and dry.

Hedge Cutting

Monday, Oct. 19th

Cross Hands, 9.00. Rode Warrior, Mabel Lancer.

Found on Adlestrop Hill, ran round about Adlestrop and Daylesford, and I think killed one fox. Ground much softer after about ¼ inch of rain in the night.

Friday, Oct. 23rd

Bourton Wood. Rode Kruger, Mabel Lancer.

Spent most of the morning in Bourton Wood and Batsford, hunting all the time. Went eventually to Cadley Arbour where we found, ran through Rook Hill, a few fields out the other side and lost.

Monday, Oct. 26th

Kineton Thorns. N. Cotswold. Rode Warrior, Mabel Lancer.

Did not draw Kineton Thorns on account of shooting. Found near Guiting Quarries and had a very nice hunt round about Trafalgar, Rook's Pool and Hinchwick, going a great pace every now and then on a very catchy scent, and finally marked him to ground in Sezincote Warren. A tremendous lot of jumping.

Mother greeting Hunt at Guiting Grange

Friday, Oct. 30th

Farmington Grove. Rode Warrior, Mabel Lancer.

Found in Farmington Grove and went away at once towards Sherborne Cow Pastures, going slowly as far as there; then, without going into the covert, ran very fast to Barrington where they checked, then right-handed up to Barrington New Inn and across the road; then right-handed again and killed on the Burford — Northleach road about ¾-mile from Barrington New Inn. A very nice run and hounds hunted most beautifully. Practically no jumping but plenty of galloping.

---

17 DAYS CUBBING; WARRIOR 8, KRUGER 8.

Monday, Nov. 2nd

Heythrop. Rode Kruger, Mabel Mrs Brassey's Nun.

Mabel and I and Kruger and Spragg *(presumably the groom)* stayed at Heythrop. A typical opening meet, plenty of foxes and not much scent. Spent most of the day running round at Heythrop, at last got away from the Kennel Plantations ran to Sandford Park and at last killed a fox in Coneygree. A poor little farmer's boy had his leg kicked and very badly broken.

STOW-ON-THE-WOLD

Wednesday, Nov. 4th

Stow-on-the-Wold. Rode Warrior, Mabel Lancer.

Found in Slaughter Copse and killed by Slaughter Gas House. Found in Osier bed below Upper Slaughter Manor, ran up to Captain Brassey's new cover, then down the hill again, up past Swiss Cottage, by Copse Hill, and up again to Captain Brassey's new covers and lost. Found near Swell Wold, ran out as far as Brockhill Clump, then towards Slaughter and lost. Found a tired fox in osier bed by Cress Cottage, ran up to the new covers again, then back and killed by Eyford House.

Thursday, Nov. 5th

Guiting Grange. N. Cotswold. Rode Kruger, Mother Bogy.

Found in Guiting Brake and went away at once from the top end; ran very fast past the top of the park, through Lark Wood, Craven Wood and Lee Wood, by Temple Guiting, through Waterloo Larches and lost near Pinnock. While we were drawing Kineton Thorns, fox was halloaed away towards Guiting Quarries, but hounds could make nothing of it. Found close to Guiting Quarries, ran a very fast circle of 10 minutes and killed close to where we found. I was given the brush as a polite little acknowledgement to mother for welcoming the hounds at Guiting — I am quite sure!

Thursday, Nov. 12th

Blockley. N. Cotswold. Rode Warrior.

Found, and after running round Northwick Park two or three times, killed in a barn. Did not find again till Churnell, where after hanging about for some time the fox went away towards Middle Hill, and hounds were whipped off after crossing the Broadway road on account of shooting. Very dull day.

Friday, Nov. 13th

New Barn. Rode Kruger, Mabel Lancer, Mother Bogy.

Found in Lodge Park, ran a fast but very small circle, dragged on for some time and lost. Found in larch cover above Sherborne House, ran fast into Farmington Grove, out right-handed towards Sherborne Cow Pastures, then left-handed below Clapton village, left again just short of Clapton Gorse, up the hill nearly to Gilbert's Grave, then left-handed again back into Farmington Grove, and slowly out the other side towards Sherborne. We came home. Not at all a bad day and Kruger was going very nicely. Mother was nearly run away with as her curb chain broke, a brand new one.

Mother nearly run away with
when her curb chain broke

Tuesday, Nov. 17th

Temple Guiting. N. Cotswold. Rode Warrior, Mabel Lorna Doone, Sophie Clonmel, Mother Bogy.

Found in Lee Wood, ran slowly through Guiting Quarries on to Hornsleasow covers and lost. Found again near Lee Wood and to ground close to Temple Guiting. Drew Guiting Quarries and Trafalgar covers blank. Found an outlying fox in a turnip field near Rook's Pool; ran very fast for about 10 minutes and killed close to Fox Farm.

Wednesday, Nov. 18th

Gawcomb. Rode Kruger, Mabel Lancer.

Found in Gawcomb; ran very well below Icomb, left Icomb Cow Pastures on our right, checked for a minute in the road, then on just to the right of Oddington Lower Ashes, across to the lower end of Oddington Lower Ashes and killed. Fox jumped up close by and ran across the river and the line to Kingham, then hunted on slowly to Sarsgrove and lost. Trotted all the way back to Icomb Cow Pastures which was blank as were also Maugersbury Grove and Botany Bay. Found in Wyck Hill Kennel Copse ran back into Gawcomb where they stayed about and did not do any more.

Friday, Nov. 20th

Moreton-in-Marsh. Rode Warrior, Mabel Lorna Doone, Sophie Clonmel, Mother Bogy.

Frogmore blank. Found in Crawthornes but he was a bad fox and would not run straight and there was not much scent. Mrs Thursby's covers blank.

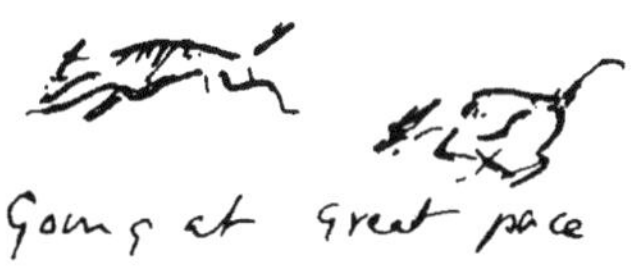

Mr Pritchard found a fox and halloaed him away from above Donnington; they ran him through the privet cover and to ground in Banks Fee Park. Found in Mrs Godman's Windmill cover, ran back over the hill and down into the vale between Banks Fee and Donnington; then turned short left-handed up the hill again, down past Donnington Brewery, right-handed by the Windmill cover, then left-handed to Hensgrove, then back again towards Condicote when we came home. Mabel and I stayed at Banks Fee.

Monday, Nov. 23rd

Chapel House. Rode Kruger, Mabel Lancer, Sophie Clonmel, Mother Bogy.

Horses came on by the early train (*from Notgrove station presumably)* and we motored. Found in Walk Gorse, ran round Badger's Gorse, nearly back to Walk Gorse, then left-handed into Heythrop Park, through the Ovens, hung about by the house for a bit, then out at the far end through Henley Knapp and finally marked him to ground near Tracey's Farm. They ran very fast and well from Heythrop to Henley Knapp. Trotted back to Salford Osiers where they found and ran back in the direction of Heythrop. We left them as our horses had to catch the 4.45 train. A wonderfully good scent considering that there was a very high wind.

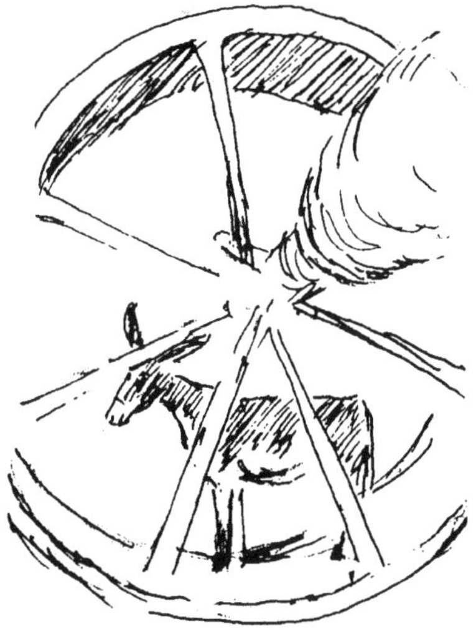

DONNINGTON BREWERY

Friday, Nov. 27th

Bourton-on-the-Water. Rode Warrior, Mabel Lancer, Sophie Clonmel, Mother Bogy.

Found in larch cover above Bourton Bridge, ran a few fields and killed; went on after another fox through Clapton Gorse, down nearly to the river and killed; spinnies by Bourton blank. Found in Redesdale's, ran up over the hill by Lower Slaughter, through Stow Bridge Copse into Wyck Hill Kennel Copse, then turned short back and killed him by the Copse Hill Lower Lodge. On our way to draw covers round Leygore a fox halloaed above Redesdale's Gorse, but hounds could make nothing of it. Found in a long plantation near Turkdean, ran to Farmington Grove. Hounds were then taken back to kill a fox found sitting in the middle of a field with a trap on one of its forelegs. Horrible. A great deal of wire about.

Saturday, Nov. 28th

Hawling Downs. Cotswold. Rode Kruger.

Found an outlying fox not far from Gazely; ran a few fields well, then dragged slowly on somewhere out by Roel Gate and nearly down to Andoversford. Found in Lawrence's Gorse, ran to Salperton and eventually killed near Notgrove station, more by good luck than anything else. Gazely blank. A poor day; a weird field and a great deal of wire.

Wednesday, Dec. 2nd

Chipping Norton Junction. Rode Warrior, Mabel Lancer, Mother Bogy.

Horses arrive at the Junction (Kingham)

Horses trained from Notgrove to the junction. Found in Bould Wood, ran very fast out to Tangley where, after running round about for some time and going out towards Barrington, we lost. Went back to draw Bruern where we found 2 foxes, one of which was supposed to go to Shipton, but I don't think that the main pack of the hounds ever spoke to the line, though one hound did have a line about 3 fields ahead. Came back to Bruern again, and found; ran up to Tangley over exactly the same line as in the morning. We then came home. There was a very good scent on the grass and if only foxes had taken better lines we should have had a better run — I think.

Friday, Dec. 4th

Moreton-in-Marsh. Rode Kruger, Mabel Lorna Doone.

Found in Rook Hill; ran by Aston Magna, twisted about the side of the hill below Cadley Arbour for some time, then crossed the railway line, and finally lost not far from Blockley. Found in Bourton Wood, ran fast along the bottom to Cadley Arbour, stayed about there for some time, then got away close to a fox which went straight to Bourton Wood and on through Northwick Park, turned right-handed without going into Sedgecomb and to within a few fields of Blockley station, where scent unaccountably failed. A good run over bad country. A very wet stormy day, which had an evil effect upon Kruger's temper.

"Deep going"

Monday, Dec. 7th

Ledwell Village. Stayed at Ranger's Lodge and rode Warrior.

Found in Worton Heath, ran into Ledwell village and lost. Went back to Worton Heath, found again, ran to ground near Nether Worton. A thick fog came on. We found in a gorse and ran very intermittently to near Barton; owing to the fog we went to Tew where it was fairly clear and drew Conygree, Tew Gardens and Tew Pond Tail, all of which were blank. A very bad day.

Wednesday, Dec. 9th

Adlestrop. Rode Kruger, Mabel Lancer.

Found on Adlestrop Hill; ran a circle round by Daylesford and hung about the hill a bit and to ground by Chastleton. Found in the Harcombs; went away at the bottom ran very well for a few fields; turned right-handed just short of Evenlode Mains, up by the side of Kitebrook, when scent seemed practically to fail, but Sturman cast them on up to Chastleton and to the Harcombs, where there seemed a line out at the bottom, but it soon failed and they returned to Chastleton where they ate the fox which had been previously run to ground. Chastleton Grove blank. Evenlode Mains blank; found in osier bed near railway and started away very well, but scent soon failed. Found again near the same place and again started away very well and thought we were going to have a great run, but scent failed and we finally gave it up near Condicote Farm. A very disappointing day, but enjoyable as there was lots doing all the time and plenty of jumping, and many falls. K. Freer had the shaft of a cart run into the shoulder of her horse. Fortunately no permanent injury, but it will be laid up for some time. We had a great many fairly small open ditches to jump which were excellent for Kruger's education.

Friday, Dec. 11th

Farmington Grove. Rode Warrior, Mabel Lorna Doone, Mother Bogy.

A very bad day. Found in Farmington Grove, Sherborne Osiers and Clapton Gorse.

"a very wet stormy day which had an evil effect on Kruger's temper."

Monday, Dec. 14th

Boulter's Barn. Rode Kruger, Mabel Lancer.

Found in Sarsgrove; ran out nearly to Churchill and lost. Found again in Sarsgrove and killed not far from Sarsden House, a mangy fox. *(Mange was rife among foxes over much of the country in the latter part of the 19th century)*. Churchill Heath blank. Found in Bould Wood and the fox broke away at the Gawcomb end, but instead of going, as we hoped, straight up the vale for Gawcomb, turned off left-handed up the hill, then right-handed along the edge, nearly to Westcote; then hounds got muddled amongst the cottages and farm buildings and finally gave it up. Bogy had his foot bruised by his shoe at Farmington and is lame.

Tuesday, Dec. 15th

Naunton. N. Cotswold. Rode Warrior.

Naunton Spinney blank. Found in turnip field close by; ran through Guiting Park and lost. Drew Guiting Brake, but hounds did not find though a fox was seen. Lark Wood, Craven and Lee Wood blank. Found above Temple Guiting and killed near Guiting Quarries. Did not find again while I was out. A very bad day.

Friday, Dec. 18th

Stow-on-the-Wold. Rode Warrior, Mabel Lancer, Mother Kruger.

A really good day, the best I have had from Stow. Found in Swell Osiers; ran across the Evesham road, right-handed across the Moreton road cutting *(No Man's Land)*, right-handed again above Broadwell Hill, past Marjorie Coppice, left Maugersbury Grove on the right, and killed in the ditch just below Gawcomb.

Going to the Meet

Lead horse to be hunted by one of the Ladies

They simply raced and Sturman never got up with them till close to Maugersbury Grove, where Mabel and I also got up to them. Nobody was really with them, Will and Mr Barnsley were the nearest. Found in Slaughter Copses, ran to ground in Mr Cheetham's slate quarries. Found in Captain Brassey's larch cover, ran over the hill across Aston brook and through Redesdale's Gorse towards Cold Aston; turned left-handed and crossed the Northleach road to Clapton Gorse, then back again and killed not far from where they found. We came home before the end as the horses had had a very hard day.

Being "mounted" side-saddle

Wednesday, Dec. 23rd

Bradwell Grove. Rode Warrior, Sophie Kruger, Mabel Lancer.

The horses were sent on to New Barn the day before. Drew for some time without finding, but at last found near Patcat Gorse and had a long run, which was of a rather disappointing nature as we got out of our country and into a country of many small coverts, where hounds would run well for about two fields and then check, and so on. Finally gave it up, but on our way back to draw we came upon an apparently hunted fox who finally landed us at Hatherop.

Second horseman were the lightest of the Stableboys. They were expected to keep up with the hunt and jump if necessary

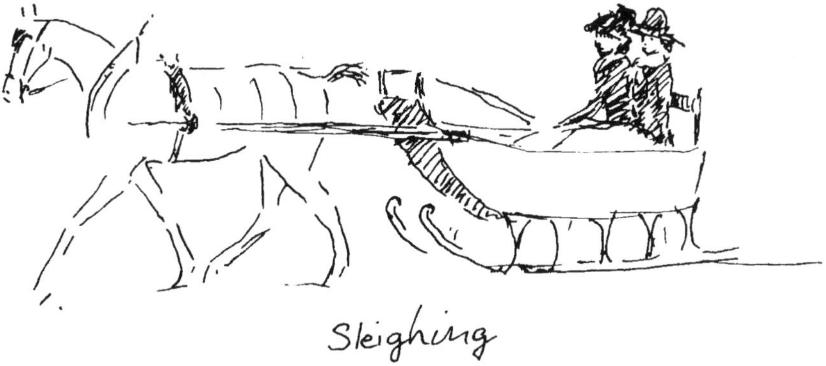

Saturday, Jan. 2nd

The Kennels. North Cotswold. Rode Warrior.

I had frost nails put in to get to Broadway but had them taken out there as the ice was very quickly thawing from the road. There was a good deal of snow where it had drifted, but it had gone in the most extraordinary way, as on Wednesday and Tuesday there was nearly a foot of snow and the sleigh went very well. We spent the whole day on the side of the hill between Buckland Wood and Lidcomb Wood and there were plenty of foxes but not a good scent, and I came home early thoroughly bored!

Monday, Jan. 4th

Heythrop. Rode Kruger, Mabel Lorna Doone, Mother Bogy.

Spent the whole day running about Heythrop. A good scent was wasted on bad foxes who would not run straight.

Wednesday, Jan. 6th

Merrymouth. Rode Warrior, Mabel Lancer.

Tangley and Taynton Quarries blank. Found in Barrington Bushes, ran all about Tangley and Taynton Quarries and finally lost in Tangley. Found near Rissington Common, ran past Little Rissington village then right-handed to Tangley when I came home. It was a nice, fast, little gallop and redeemed an otherwise bad day.

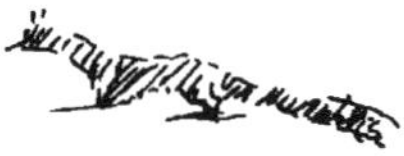

Friday, Jan. 8th

Moreton. Rode Kruger.

Bogy and Lorna Doone both a little tender after Monday, owing to bad shoeing by the Guiting blacksmith who has been cutting their feet down too low. Warrior is also lame from corns. We have now changed back to Betteridge.

Thickleather and Blackthorns blank. Found close to Sezincote House ran to ground in the Woodpits. Found in Banks Fee beech cover, ran up behind Donnington, then left-handed down the hill across Tump Ground; then left-handed again up through Banks Fee Garden and then slowly with many checks through the Windmill cover right-handed through Dibden's Gorse and Hensgrove, then back to Banks Fee, where they began to run really well and slipped away round the bottom of Tump Ground, down into the vale, crossed the Longborough road and on to Sezincote, where scent was again bad and after going to within a field of Bourton Wood cast down into the vale by Sezincote Lower Lodge where they gave it up. We then drew Frogmore and found, and I came home as they did not seem to be coming my way. It was very heavy going in the vale.

Warrior telescopes Tall hat. It's fallen off & he jumps on it.

Monday, Jan. 11th

Boulter's Barn. Rode Warrior, Mabel Lancer.

Found in Sarsgrove, ran out towards Chipping Norton, having killed a fox in Sarsgrove, then left-handed and marked him to ground in roadside drain below Boulter's Barn. Found and killed close to Sarsden House. Found in the Norrels, ran out the Ascott side, but soon turned right-handed and crossed the line and brook and into Bruern, out the other side and through Milton and Shipton and to ground between Shipton and Ascott. Found in Churchill Heath ran into Bould Wood and marked him to ground in rough furzy field on the Idbury side. I spoilt my tall hat.
It fell off going through a fence and then Warrior telescoped it by putting his foot bang on top of the crown! Lamed Warrior.

Tuesday, Jan. 12th

Hinchwick. N. Cotswold. Rode Kruger, Mabel Lorna Doone.

Sezincote Warren blank. Found in Beechy Bank, ran into Springhill, spent some time there and then ran on into Middle Hill where they eventually gave him up. Found in Hornsleasow ran in the direction of Snowshill. I came home as I wanted Kruger again for Friday.

Warrior lame

Saturday, Jan. 16th

New Barn. Rode Kruger, Mabel Lancer & Lorna Doone, Mother Bogy.

Lodge Park cover blank. Found in Broadfield Plantation, ran well for about 3 fields then dragged on for ever so long with hardly any line at all. Found in Farmington Grove and killed down by the brook. Picked up the line of another fox ran through Sherborne Park and lost. Found in Sherborne Cow Pastures and lost by Clapton village when I came home.

Wednesday, Jan. 20th

Stow Station. Rode Kruger, Mabel Lorna Doone.

Stow Bridge Copse blank; (they were at work in it). Found in Kennel Copse, ran through Gawcomb and slowly across the vale to Bould Wood where we ran round for some time. Drew Icomb Cow Pastures and Oddington Upper Ashes blank. Found in Maugersbury Grove, ran round about and finally lost by the railway below Maugersbury Grove.

Wednesday, Feb. 3rd

Bledington. Rode Kruger, Mabel Lorna Doone, Mother Bogy.

Found in Oddington Ashes ran rather slowly across to Oddington Upper Ashes, then towards Maugersbury Grove but turned left-handed and into Gawcomb, out at the top and into Wyck Hill, along a few fields towards Little Rissington then back again into Gawcomb, out at the bottom and to Icomb and lost. Found in Maugersbury Grove, ran into Gawcomb, when we came home.

Friday, Feb. 5th

Stow-on-the-Wold. Rode Warrior & Bachelor, Mabel Lancer.

Found in small cover above Lower Swell and ran across the Eyford road to the upper road to Slaughter and checked; then hounds were lifted on to the line and ran by the green ride, through Upper Slaughter, over the hill, down across the brook by Aston Mill, then left-handed down the brook to Bourton Bridge, crossed the line and left-handed again by the side of the road up to Stow Bridge Copse; quickly through and very fast up to Copse Hill and on into the Eyford covers, where, after they thought they had lost him, he was viewed, and they killed him in the green ride. *(This would be what is now called the Hollow, running from Swiss Farm to Hollow Barn)*. He must have been the hunted fox as he was quite stiff. I changed on to Bachelor and they found in Captain Brassey's larch cover, ran across Aston brook, and lost close to Cold Aston. Warrior was lame next day.

Churchill Church Tower is a copy of Magalen College (Oxford) Tower. It is the centre of the Heythrop Hunt

"Rode The Little's Badger"

Monday, Feb. 8th

Boulter's Barn. Rode Kruger, Mabel Lorna Doone, Mother Bogy.

Found in Sarsgrove; ran nearly to Churchill, then right-handed and dragged slowly on across the Cornwell — Boulter's Barn road, past the Kennels, close to Salford and finally gave it up near the Cross Hands — Rollright road. Went back and drew the Norrels where we found, ran out towards Kingham, then right-handed and slowly nearly up to the Kennels where he was marked to ground. Next we drew Churchill Heath, ran up to Sarsgrove, where we left them to catch the 4.45 train at the junction. Not a good scent.

I don't think I have ever ridden such a good Horse

Wednesday, Feb. 10th

Ledwell Village. Stayed with the Meyricks for Heythrop Ball; rode Stockings.

Found in Worton Heath, ran slowly out to Barton and lost. Found in osier bed near North Aston, ran fast for a few minutes to Dean Hill after which they could not make much more of it. Drew all the covers up the brook to Hawk Hill blank. Then drew Iron Down blank and went home. A rotten day and latterly pouring wet and cold.

Saturday, Feb. 13th

Evenlode. Rode the Littles' Badger, Mabel Lorna Doone.

The nicest day I have had this season — Evenlode Mains blank. Found in osier bed nearby, ran fast for a field or two then slowly and into Evenlode Mains, then a very fast few fields and lost. Found in the Harcombs, ran round the side of the hill nearly to Adlestrop station, then right-handed along the Evenlode, and nearly to Crawthornes; the fox, with a few hounds, had however crossed the Evenlode and gone to Mrs Thursby's cover, so Will found out his mistake and went after them. Hounds got away pretty close to their fox from Mrs Thursby's cover, ran well up over the hill by Marjorie Copse down to the railway bridge, then simply raced across the bit of

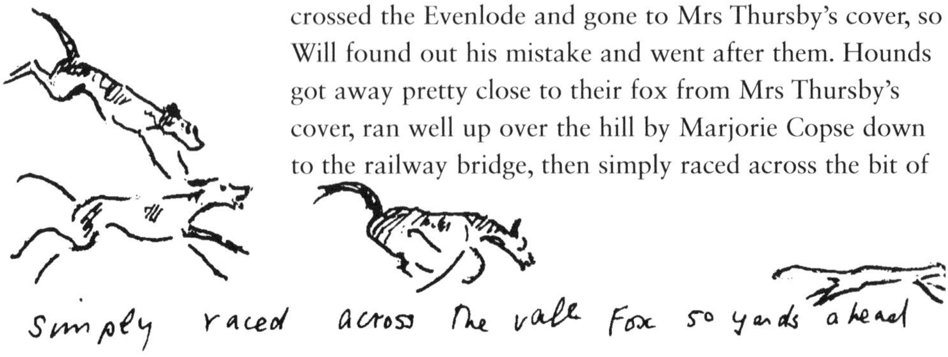
simply raced across the vale Fox 50 yards ahead

vale to Oddington Ashes, with the fox only about 50 yards ahead, and they ran him up into the rick yard by the Rectory and after that could not do any more. I think he stayed in the rick yard, but Will blew them out and put them on to a line which took them out to the railway bridge, after which they lost. Found on Adlestrop Hill, ran down into the Neats then through the Harcombs, and very fast over a nice bit of vale nearly to Little Compton, then turned right-handed up on to Chastleton Hill and across the road to Daylesford where they lost. Mine was such a good mount and carried me most awfully well — I don't think I have ever ridden such a good horse. Will must have been pleased with his day and he did awfully well but it was bad luck that he did not kill either of his foxes.

Mr Oakley had a fall

Wednesday, Feb. 17th

Heythrop. (Sturman hunting again). Stayed at Over Norton and rode Rex, Mabel Lancer, Mother Bogy.

A bad day. Rather good foxes but a bad scent. The day ended tragically as Mr Oakley *(of Chadlington)* had a fall over a wall and broke his back. They could not get him home for ages and then were not sure for 2 or 3 days what he had done. The wall is near Heythrop Banbury Lodge; a small wall into some cart ruts, which we have jumped many times, and we all jumped it then. He broke his back and only lived about a fortnight.

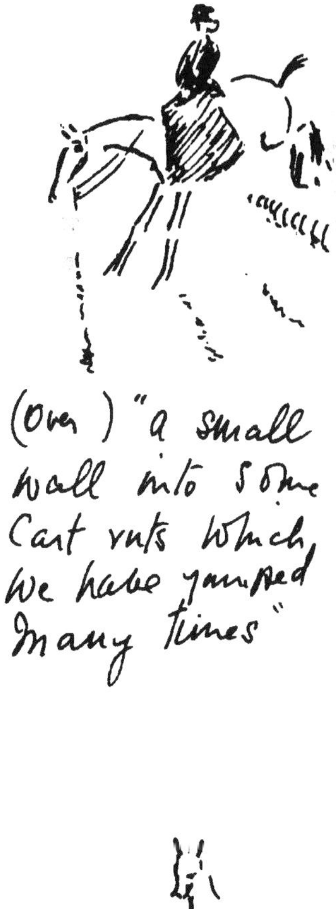
(Over) "a small wall into some Cart ruts which we have jumped many times"

Friday, Feb. 19th

Burford. Rode Kruger, Mabel Lorna Doone.

Hounds did not meet till 12 on account of the frost, and then it was not really fit. Found in Windrush Poor Lots, ran to the small cover on Bibury race course, then left-handed very fast to Jolly's Gorse and killed by some buildings a few fields away. Found in gorse near Jolly's, ran to Barrington, twisted round about there a long time and at last killed in the middle of the village.

Stopped by frost and snow. We had as much as 27 degrees of frost and 8 inches of snow.

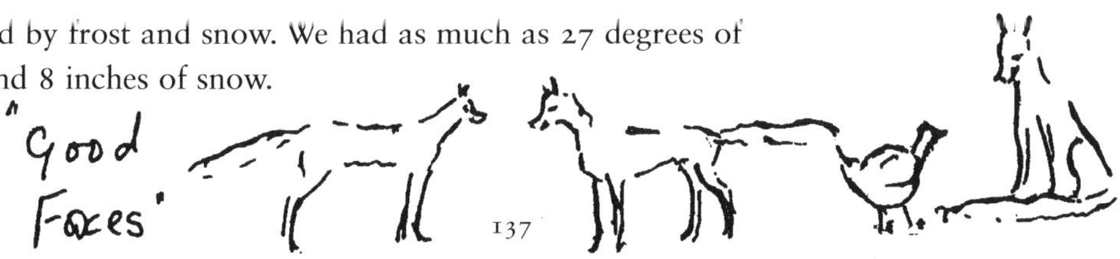
"Good Foxes"

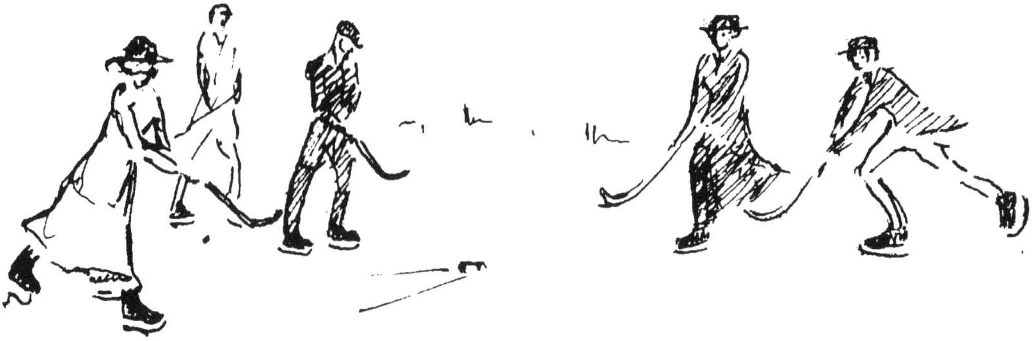

Ice hockey on the lake at Upper Slaughter Manor

Saturday, March 13th

Toddington Station. N. Cotswold. Rode Warrior, Mabel Lorna Doone, Mother Bogy.

It was still quite unfit to hunt on the hills on account of the snow, but down in the vale it was quite clear. A bad day so long as we were out. I came home early as it was Warrior's first day after his sprained hind suspensory ligament.

FROST RETURNED AGAIN FOR A FEW DAYS

Friday, March 19th

Moreton-in-Marsh. Rode Kruger & Warrior, Mabel Lancer & Lorna Doone, Mother Bogy.

Frogmore blank. Crawthornes blank. Found in Jubilee Plantation but could do nothing. Found in Crab Orchard, ran nearly to the Fish Pond Copse then back and into Crawthornes, ran straight through and very nicely into Mrs Thursby's covers, then more slowly and lost at Abbotswood, Rather nice. Found in Mrs Godman's Windmill cover ran towards Condicote then right-handed, by Dibden's Bank. A terrific rain storm came on and we lost him.

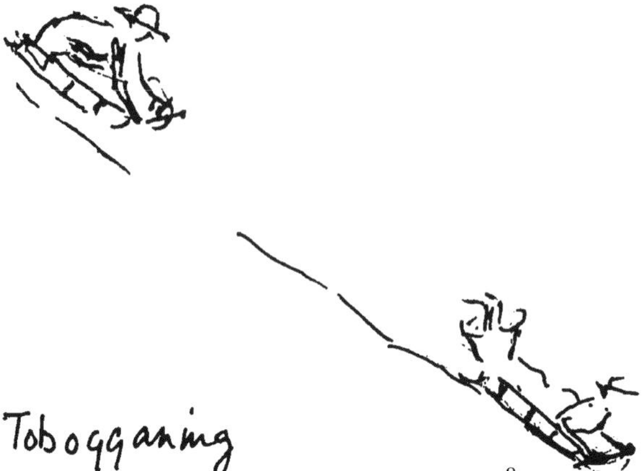

Tobogganing

Badger bought from
Col. Little for £165

Monday, March 22nd

Chapel House. Rode Badger, Mabel Lorna Doone, Mother Bogy.

Mother has given me Badger instead of Warrior, who does not seem inclined to stand very sound. She bought Badger from Colonel Little for £165. I don't think I could want a much better horse. Found in Salford Osiers and ran up on to the hill near Rollright Stones and lost. Adlestrop Hill and the Neats blank. Found in the Harcombs, ran over the shoulder of the hill towards Adlestrop village then right-handed and to ground close to Evenlode. I had a most lucky escape over some barbed wire, as I did not see it in a hedge until too late, and Badger hit it, came down on his knees and got up again none the worse. Found in osier bed near Evenlode Mains, ran to the left of Evenlode village, then right-handed and lost near Stock Bridge. Rather a disappointing day.

Badger came down
on his knees

Wednesday, March 24th

Adderbury. Rode Kruger, Mabel Lancer.

Motored, and sent horses by train and they slept at Ranger's Lodge.

Covers by Adderbury blank. Found not very far off, ran rather nicely back to Adderbury and killed. Found two foxes in Wilson's gorse, ran one to ground immediately. Hounds were then put on to the line of the other but they could not do much with it. Dean Hill and covers by North Aston blank and hounds went home. A pouring wet day and had 26 miles to motor home wet through.

Got up again none
the worse

"26 miles to motor home wet through" (from North Aston.)

Friday, March 26th
Barrington New Inn. Rode Badger, Mabel Lorna Doone, Mother tried horse of Barton's which she has since bought. *(Three generations of Bartons have farmed at Williamstrip and dealt in hunters and more recently polo ponies).*

Windrush Poor Lots and Jolly's gorse blank. Found in gorse close by, had a fairly long run but not very exciting. They killed two foxes in the course of the day. We were on the move all day, and it was the most extraordinarily tiring day. Mother liked her horse very much, but she succeeded in knocking down an old man of the name of Jacobs. I don't think he could hold his horse.

"Mother tried Barton's Horse"

Saturday, March 27th
Kineton Thorns. N. Cotswold. Rode Warrior, Mabel Lancer.

Found in Kineton Thorns, ran into Lark and Lee Wood, whereabouts they stayed as long as I was out. Came home early so as not to give Warrior a long day. I heard the Cotswold hounds had run close by Guiting, so I got Kruger out and found them at Salperton. They found in Lawrence's Gorse and had a bit of a run, but as Kruger had not been fed for hunting I could not go.

"Which she has since Bought"

Tuesday, March 30th

Oddington. Rode Kruger & Bogy, Mabel Lorna Doone.

Found in Oddington Ashes and went away at the lower end, crossed the line, close past Icomb Cow Pastures, left-handed below Icomb, into Gawcomb and eventually lost. Stow Bridge Copse blank. Found in Wyck Hill Kennel Copse and ran towards Maugersbury Grove, then right-handed over the hill and below Gawcomb, very fast along the vale, then leaving Bould Wood a field on the left, turned up on to the hill and lost near Merrymouth. Fox must have been dead beat as the pace latterly was very fast. A good day and my two horses came in most conveniently.

Wednesday, March 31st

Farmington Grove. Rode Badger, Mabel Warrior.

A very wet day but a very good one. Did not do much till we got on a fox in a cover near Turkdean, and had a good run very fast over the walls and to ground near Hampnett.

Saturday, April 3rd

Sezincote Warren. Rode Kruger, Mabel Lorna Doone.

Monday, April 5th

Boulter's Barn. Mabel Warrior.

Wednesday, April 7th

Moreton. Rode Badger, Mabel Lorna Doone.

Heat and dust awful. I had had slight 'flu and felt rather a rag. Found in Batsford and hounds ran very fast into the vale nearly to Aston Hales then left handed by Aston Magna up onto the hill and lost. No one was really with them the first part and I was not at all. The rest of the day we did very little but ride about Bourton Wood.

"Kruger cut shin
trying to refuse
wall"

Thursday, April 8th

Ford. N. Cotswold. Rode Kruger, Mabel Lancer.

Again fearfully hot and not much of a day. On the way to find the hounds Kruger cut his shin over a wall, which he tried to refuse, and as it came up rather next day it was decided that he should finish his season. Lancer also finished his season as he was a little lame in his shoulder and is to be blistered.

Friday, April 9th

Broadway. N. Cotswold. Mabel rode Warrior.

"Kruger finished season"

Monday, April 12th

Chipping Norton Junction. Rode Warrior, Mabel Lorna Doone, Sophie Badger.

Found in Oddington Ashes ran out towards the Upper Ashes. Killed down in the vale below Idbury after a very good hunting run of about 2 hours.

Friday, April 16th

New Barn. Rode Badger, Mabel Lorna Doone.

Not much of a day to finish the season.

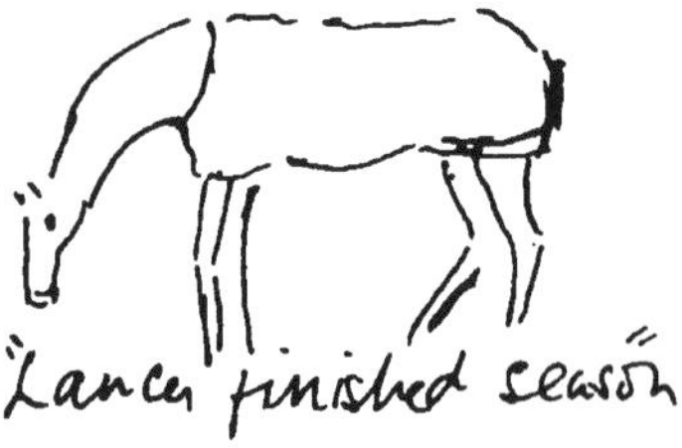
"Lancer finished season"

May

Ivy Bridge. Dartmoor Hounds. Rode the Cornishman, stayed at Sandwell.

Not a good but an enjoyable day up on the moors.

May

Wrangaton. Dartmoor Hounds. Rode Pandora.

A bad day with very few foxes and a horrid wind. But it was very clear and there were most glorious views.

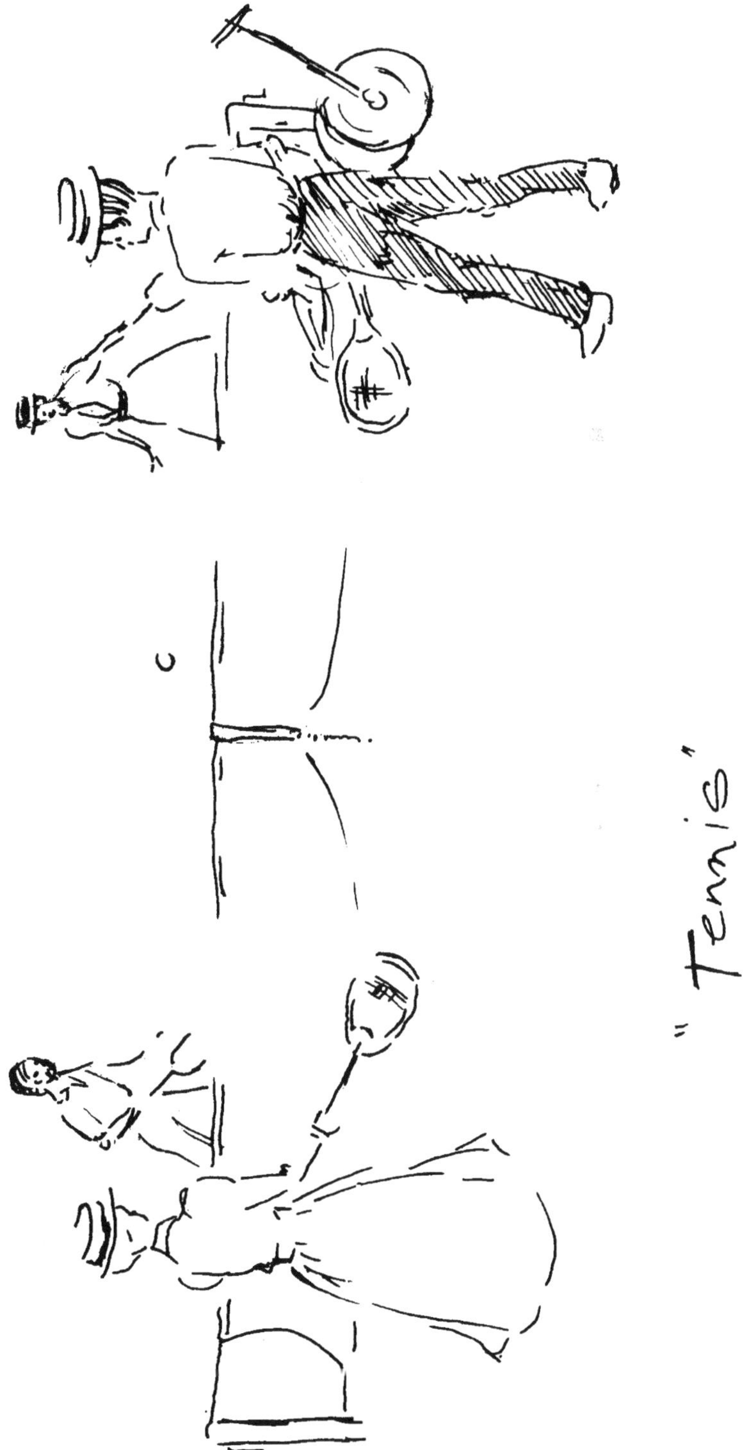
"Tennis"

Jack Kennard
rode Mrs Hank's
Bay, late R. Freer's

SEASON 1909-1910

Saturday, Sep. 18th

Bruern. Rode Kruger, Mabel Lancer.

Friday, Sep. 24th

Crawthornes. Rode Badger, Mabel Lancer, Jack Kennard rode Mrs Hanks' bay, late R. Freer's.

(The appearance of Jack Kennard on the scene seems to interfere with the keeping of the diary!).

Sept.

Adlestrop. Rode Kruger.

Rode Kruger

Sept.

Cold Aston. Rode Badger, Mabel Lancer.

Found in Cold Aston; killed one. Foxes in Redesdale's gorse and killed two.

Oct.

Gawcomb. Rode Kruger, Mabel Lancer.

Foxes in Gawcomb, but did not kill. Killed one in Kennel Copse, Wyck Hill.

Oct.

Bourton Wood. Rode Badger.

M. Lancer

Oct.

Guiting Wood. N. Cotswold. Rode Kruger, Mabel Lancer.

Lots of foxes but could not kill till one just after we had gone home.

Oct.

Guiting Grange. N. Cotswold. Rode Badger, Mabel Lancer.

Found in Brake, but did not kill.

Oct.

Temple Guiting. N. Cotswold. Rode Kruger.

Rather a good morning but not for me! Firstly I arrived late and found them near Mrs Godman's Windmill, having run there fast from near Temple Guiting. Secondly having found in Rooks Pool I fell off when Kruger refused the second wall! Got on again and found hounds at once, only to refuse again and never got Kruger over! Found hounds again just as they went home.

"I fell off when Kruger refused second wall"

Saturday, Oct. 16th

Claverton. North Warwickshire. Rode Arkwright's Augusta and Tiger.

Bad morning but delightful mounts.

Wednesday, Oct. 20th

Foxholes. Rode Badger.

In Bould Wood and Bruern all morning and killed two foxes.

Rode Arkwright's Augusta

Friday, Oct. 22nd

Farmington Grove. Rode Kruger, Mabel Lancer.

Foxes in Farmington Grove. Found in small cover between Farmington Grove and Sherborne Cow Pastures, ran into the Grove, then out the other side, raced over about six fields and killed. Hounds went home having been out two hours.

+ Tiger, delightful mounts

Monday, Oct. 25th

Oddington. Rode Kruger, Mother hired mare.

Oddington Ashes blank. Found in Icomb Cow Pastures, ran a very fast circle by the Upper Ashes and close back by the Cow Pastures, crossed the brook by Bledington, through Bould Wood and to ground the other side. I did not see any of it.

Friday, O ct. 29th

Sezincote. Rode Mrs Little's Greyshoes.

A very dull morning on a very nice horse.

Bledington Bridge

Saturday, Oct. 30th

Guiting Quarry. N. Cotswold. Rode Badger, Mother hired mare.

Found in Guiting Quarry Cover; ran very well for a few fields but had to be stopped on account of shooting. Found Kineton Thorns, ran nearly to Pole Plantation and lost near Condicote. Very nice. Found in new larch plantation this side Lea Wood and ran very fast through Lark and Lea Woods, above Temple Guiting, and killed in Guiting Quarry.

Left!

Monday, Nov. 1st

Heythrop. Stayed at Heythrop and rode Kruger. Mabel Lancer.

Found in the Ovens, ran a bit of a circle and lost by Banbury Lodge. Found in Walk Gorse, had quite a good run and killed. I came home after they left Walk Gorse as I got a bad start and wanted Kruger again Wednesday and Badger was a little lame after Saturday.

Wednesday, Nov. 3rd

Bradwell Grove. Tried Barton's mare for mother, and had Kruger's hind fetlock very badly cut while being ridden by Barton's second horseman.

I liked the mare I was trying very much and had quite a good gallop on her, in fact young Barton was very anxious to get me off her. They found in Bradwell Grove, ran a nice circle coming back past Jolly's Gorse and lost.

Stopped on account of shooting

Friday, Nov. 5th

Stow. Rode Sophia (Little's), Mabel Lancer.

Found in Swell osiers, ran over the hill to the

bottom of Banks Fee, then sharp left-handed up the hill again to Mrs Godman's Windmill, then right-handed to the Sezincote covers, through Sezincote Warren, when Sophia could gallop no longer and I came home. They lost a mile or two beyond the Warren.

Monday, Nov. 8th

Boulter's Barn. Rode Rex *(Daly's)*, Mabel Lancer & Lorna Doone, Sophie new chestnut mare.

Found in Sarsgrove; ran round about in the most futile manner all the morning. In the afternoon found in Partridge cover, ran very well to Dean Grove, then back to Chadlington and I came home. A very cheerful finish to the day and Rex was an angel. Badger still laid up, slightly lame in front; Kruger also laid up with his cut.

"Tried Barton's Mare"

Friday, Nov. 12th

New Barn. Rode Mr Fenwick's Buckskin; Mabel Lancer and Lorna Doone; Sophie chestnut mare.

Found just outside Sherborne Lodge Park; ran very nicely for about 5 minutes to ground in a drain, bolted him out and killed him. Found in Lodge Park; ran nicely past Farmington village, up to Farmington Grove then right-handed along the bottom across by the mill, on into Sherborne Park and killed in the road above Sherborne village. Found far side of Sherborne Park, but although they got away close on their fox there was hardly any scent and soon lost him. Drew Sherborne gorse and Snowbottom Belt blank and came home. Such a good mount. Killed 5 foxes.

Liked her very much

Wednesday, Nov. 17th

Stow Station. Rode Sheila Pollok's Knap, Mabel Lorna Doone, Sophie chestnut mare.

Stow Bridge Copse and Wyck Hill blank. Found in Gawcomb, ran round by Icomb House then right-handed across the vale below Gawcomb; then right-handed again to the Rissington covers where we spent the rest of the day running from one to the other, the scent being very catchy. A very nice mount, but a bad day.

Rode Sophia (Little's)

Friday, Nov. 19th

Moreton. Rode Badger, Mabel Lancer.

Found in Frogmore, ran across the Moreton road up to Donnington and Banks Fee, stayed about there a bit, then to Crabby and back to Banks Fee again, then quite nicely across the bit of vale from the Tump Ground to Sezincote and to ground in quarry above Sezincote lane. Found in Banks Fee privet cover ran just into the vale over Tump Ground then turned back to privet cover and over the hill as if for the windmill cover but turned back to Banks Fee, when I came home as it was Badger's first day for nearly 3 weeks.

Rode Rex (Daley's)

Monday, Nov. 22nd

Chapel House. Rode Badger and chestnut mare.

Found in Walk Gorse; ran to ground close to Heythrop Banbury Lodge. A very frosty morning and I think an extra long time was spent digging in order to let it thaw. Horace's horse slipped on landing and broke Horace's collar bone. Found in Salford Gorse, ran a very small circle and killed in Salford Gorse. Found in Salford Osiers and had a good hunting run round by Mr Young's Homes and Daylesford village, over Adlestrop Hill and finally gave up on Chastleton Hill.

Friday, Nov. 26th

Farmington Grove. Rode Kruger and Cutlet, Mabel Lancer.

Found in Farmington Grove and after a longish hunting run killed in Long Plantation Leygore side of Farmington Pillars. Kruger was a perfect pig, refused most determinedly, and quite defeated me. Had rather a nice, slow, hunting run from near Farmington Grove and lost in Upper Slaughter.

"Sophia (rode) new Chestnut Mare."

Monday, Nov. 29th

Heythrop. Rode Badger, Mabel Lorna Doone.

A bad day and few foxes.

Wednesday, Dec. 1st

Bledington Mill. Rode Kruger, Mabel Sophia and Lancer.

Found in Bould Wood, circled around a bit, and at last got away to Milton and marked him to ground between Milton and Ascott. Found in Bould Wood and hunted slowly across the vale to Gawcomb and lost. Wyck Hill, Botany Bay and Maugersbury Grove blank, found in gorse close by, ran a circle by the Upper Ashes but at last got away into the vale, running close past Icomb Cow Pastures and across the vale to Bould village where we left them. They finally gave up in the dark near Churchill Heath. Kruger very good, with aid of cutting whip.

"Rode new Chestnut Mare"

Friday, Dec. 3rd

Moreton. Rode Badger, Mabel Lorna Doone, Sophie Cutlet.

Found plenty of foxes about Cadley, Batsford and Bourton Wood and killed two. Going most terribly deep and bad scent.

Monday, Dec. 6th

Guiting Wood. N. Cotswold. Rode Kruger, Mabel Lancer, Sophie Cutlet.

Spent a long time running about the wood and killed one near Bisbeach, but at last got away past Kineton village to Lark Wood then with many checks to Kineton Thorns, Trafalgar, near Sezincote Warren, Hornsleasow and gave up near Snowshill. We are supposed to have changed foxes on Guiting Hill.

"Horace's Horse broke Horace's Collar bone"

Friday, Dec. 10th

Barrington New Inn. Rode Kruger & Badger, Mabel Lancer & Lorna Doone.

Westwell and Windrush Poor Lots and Jolly's Gorse blank. Found in long gorse cover but scent bad and soon lost. Found in Patcat gorse and killed close by. Did not find again. Soaking wet day.

"Kruger perfect pig & defeated me."

Monday, Dec. 13th

Guiting Grange. N. Cotswold. Rode Badger, Mabel Lorna Doone.

The brake blank! Found Lark or Lee Wood ran by Temple Guiting and over the hill as if for Guiting Wood, but turned short back near Castlett and lost near Temple Guiting. Found again but did little. Then went to Peewit Hill and found; ran down into the vale through Lidcomb Wood and across the Vale, hounds quite alone to Great Grove where we caught them.

Wednesday, Dec. 15th

Adlestrop. Rode Kruger; Mabel Lancer.

Copse by station blank. Found in Oddington Ashes but could not do much, partly owing to people, myself among them, getting on too far. Found in Mrs Thursby's cover, ran out towards Broadwell then left-handed and up the hill above Broadwell; crossed the bottom by the Upper Lodge, left Maugersbury just on our right and killed below Marjorie Copse. A nice quick little gallop. Found in Crabby, ran very fast by Donnington, Banks Fee, Condicote and lost near Eyford House. A good run and just as hard as we could go. Kruger an angel.

"Kruger very good with aid of cutting whip"

Friday, Dec. 17th

Stow. Rode Badger, Mabel Lorna Doone, Sophie Cutlet.

Found in Slaughter Copse, ran to ground. Copse Hill osier bed and New Covers blank. Found in Beech belt above Rockcliff *(the Long Plantation)*, ran by Swell Wold, Rook's Pool, through Sezincote Warren, checked for some time by Dibden's Bank, then on to Condicote where we lost. Think it was very likely the same fox that we ran to Eyford on Wednesday. Most of the field got lost in the fog in Sezincote Warren. Mrs Godman's Windmill cover blank. Found in Swell Osiers; ran a very fast circle by Abbotswood, across the golf links then left-handed back over the Stow — Tewkesbury road, as if for Banks Fee, then left-handed circle back into Swell Osiers where we gave up on account of the fog. Colonel Savage, Captain Byngham and I were the only ones who had the luck to keep with them in the fog.

Saturday, Dec. 24th

Barrington Park. Rode Kruger, Sophie Badger, Mabel Lorna Doone.

Found in cover just outside Barrington Park; ran across the park and out by Taynton and lost. Rissington Common blank.

"Hounds not coming well to Sir John Campbell"

Mrs. Fenwick had rather a nasty fall over a gate

Found close by, ran towards Wyck Rissington then turned right-handed up over the hill and down through Gawcomb; then left-handed up through the Icomb cover, over the hill and down through Maugersbury Grove, across the line to Quar Wood where we checked some time but picked up the line near the Hyde, and hunted on nearly into Stow Bridge Copse, but turned right-handed and up through Copse Hill and we left them by Grannie's Bank having about lost their fox. Quite enough for one horse as it was very fast to Quar Wood and very deep going. Kruger starting a slight cough.

Wednesday, Dec. 29th

Gawcomb. Rode Badger, Mabel Lorna Doone.

Found in Gawcomb; ran round a bit, but at last got away at the bottom; ran by Bould village, turned left-handed within a field of Bould Wood; ran into Churchill Heath, when I think we changed, and went on again nearly to Churchill, but turned right-handed, ran through the Norrels and up over the hill nearly to Pudlicote; then left-handed and hunted rather slowly back past Churchill, into Churchill Heath and I left them trying to catch their fox in Bruern. A very good day. Mrs Fenwick had a rather nasty fall over a gate.

Friday, Dec. 31st

Bourton-on-the-Water. Rode Kruger, Mabel Lancer, Sophie hireling of Byard's.

Found at once by Bourton Bridge, ran up right-handed over the hill and down to Lower Slaughter, Upper Slaughter, Copse Hill and just into the Eyford covers; then turned short back and to within a field of Stow Bridge Copse; then left-handed nearly into Quar Wood; then right-handed and killed in Maugersbury. Went back to Redesdale's Gorse where we did not find. Found in boundary cover not far from Notgrove and spent the rest of the afternoon running round those hills, very fast some of the time, and I can't think why we did not catch our fox; he was quite close in front some of the time, but he was a fearful dodger.

A very hard day for the horses, very deep in the morning and fearful hills in the afternoon.

Monday, Jan. 3rd

Boulter's Barn. Rode Badger, Mabel Lorna Doone.

Found in Sarsgrove, ran out towards the Kennels and lost. Rest of the Sarsden covers blank. Found in the Norrels, ran nearly up to Churchill then left-handed through Churchill Heath and killed in Fifield Heath. Found in Bould Wood and after running round a bit got away at the Fifield end and raced up over the hill to Barrington Bushes; then left-handed through Tangley to Taynton Quarries, then back into Tangley and finally whipped off as they were leaving Barrington Bushes.

Tuesday, Jan. 4th

Temple Guiting. N. Cotswold. Rode Kruger, Mabel Lancer.

Found at once in little cover close to village; ran by Pinnock, through Guiting Wood, out by Wood Farm, right-handed out into the Cotswold country into a thick fog so that I don't know where we went till we found ourselves in Gazely; and then on into Guiting Brake where they lost and we came home. A very nice hunt indeed of about an hour; only Mabel and I and 5 others including a whip got away from Guiting Wood, so hounds were never helped at all till they got to Gazely where Mr Scott joined us.

Friday, Jan. 7th

Evenlode. Rode Badger & Kruger, Mabel Lorna Doone.

Found in osier bed near Evenlode Mains *(Yell's osiers)* and hunted slowly round by Evenlode village through Evenlode Mains and at last into Wolford Wood; hunted slowly through and a nice little circle out the other side leaving most of the field in Wolford. Finally lost in Wolford Wood. Found a fox in Chastleton Grove but he seemed to have no scent at all and we lost him immediately.

"Quite a cheerful little gallop"

Found in the Harcombs; ran a small circle in the vale and back to the Harcombs and lost. A disappointing day, not a good scent and a most disgusting fog on the hills. The little bit out beyond Wolford was very nice. Badger has a nasty cough.

"Home contented"

Monday, Jan. 10th

Hinchwick. Rode Badger, Mabel Lancer.

Found at once in long cover running down to Rook's Pool, ran fast to just the other side of Stayt's Gorse. Went to a fox halloaed from Sezincote Warren; ran nearly up to Hornsleasow Farm, then turned short left-handed, ran over Guiting Hill, across Stow — Tewkesbury road to lower end of Kineton Thorns, where they lost. A good gallop and quite enough for one horse and Badger was not very fit after his cough and made a lot of noise.

"Kruger had bad colic"

Wednesday, Jan. 12th

Langston Arms. Rode Kruger, Mabel Lorna Doone.

About two inches of snow here but much better in the vale round about Kingham. The best run this season. Found at once in Bould Wood; ran out through Bruern, turned left-handed just short of Milton; ran back into Bould Wood, through Herbert's Heath straight through and into Churchill Heath; turned short back by the station into Bould Wood; straight through and out at the Fifield end; turned short right-handed and ran down the vale past Icomb Cow Pastures as if for Oddington Ashes, but bore left-handed and checked a little in Upper Oddington, then went on below Mrs Thursby's cover and scent unaccountably failed a few fields short of Crawthornes. A splendid hunt and very fast.

"Kruger got a bit of an over-reach"

The going was perfectly fearful and horses had had quite enough. Bijou and Mr Arkwright at Heythrop for a few weeks' hunting and both much to the fore. Bijou on Clumber. Kruger got a bit of an overreach but I hope not much.

Friday, Jan. 14th

Farmington Grove. Rode Badger, Mabel Lancer, Mother Velocity.

Chopped a fox in the grove. Found by Farmington Pillars; ran as if for Turkdean, there left-handed and lost near Northleach. I saw nothing of it as I took a bad turn and could not get to them again. Aston Grove and covers about there blank. I then went home as Badger is not very fit having been off his feed with his cough. They found in Clapton Gorse and had a good run which brought them nearly to Lark Wood.

Monday, Jan. 17th

Chapel House. Rode Badger, Mabel Lorna Doone.

Found in Walk Gorse; ran into Heythrop where we hunted about some time and at last slipped away very quickly from close to the house; ran by Tew Pond Tail, Cow Hill then scent gradually failed and we finally lost by Hawk Hill. We then trotted all the way back to draw Salford Osiers where they did not find. Colonel Railston got concussion with his horse coming down in a rabbit-holey field by Walk Gorse. Rather bad concussion and not to hunt again this season.

Friday, Jan. 21st

Moreton. Rode Badger; Mabel Lancer & Lorna Doone, Mother Velocity.

A most unpleasant day for me. I tried to ride Kruger to the meet, but by the time we had reached Kineton Thorns he had very bad colic and I had very great difficulty in getting home. He poured with perspiration. About 12.30 I started out on Bogy to find hounds and Badger, *(who was presumably waiting for her with a 2nd horseman)* which I was a long time doing. They had a bit of a run and killed their fox before I got to them. They found at Banks Fee but did not do much and ground was frosty and slippery. Average day.

Monday, Jan. 24th

Lyne's Barn. N. Cotswold. Rode Kruger, Mabel Lancer.

Started rather late and found Kruger was not feeling right, but went on and came on the Cotswold by mistake; left them and found the North Cotswold in Guiting Wood where we remained. Kruger got worse and I brought him home. A very bad day.

"fairly small open ditches --- excellent for Kruger's education"

Friday, Feb. 4th

Moreton. Rode Badger & Brenda, Mabel Lancer & Lorna Doone, Mother Velocity.

Still a good deal of frost in the ground and going bad. Found foxes in Bourton Wood and Blackthorns but did no good. Frogmore and Crawthornes blank. Found in larch cover, ran up to Donnington, right-handed past Banks Fee House, through Longborough, then left-handed over the hill as if for Dibden's Bank; but turned left-handed again and marked him to ground in Mrs Godman's quarry. Quite a cheerful little gallop and sent one home contented. An average day.

Saturday, Feb. 5th

Salperton / Dumbleton. Cotswold / N.Cotswold. Rode Kruger.

Went to the meet at Salperton but hounds did not hunt on account of frost. Trotted off to find North Cotswold at Dumbleton. Found them about 3 o'clock near Toddington. Found in Toddington osier bed, hunted round gardens and at last killed in a brook close by. Very bad day.

"I had to leave (hounds) for Kruger to catch 4.45 "train"

Monday, Feb. 7th

Kineton Village. N. Cotswold. Rode Badger, Mabel Lorna Doone, Mother Brenda.

Spent morning in Guiting Wood, afternoon drawing Lark and Lee Wood, Guiting Quarries and Trafalgar blank. Very bad day.

Tuesday, Feb. 8th

Merrymouth. Rode Kruger, Mabel Lancer, Mother Velocity.

Found in Taynton Quarries and lost by Taynton village. Found in Tangley but did not do much. Drew a few Rissington covers blank. Found in Gawcomb, ran back to Tangley. Bad day.

Friday, Feb. 11th

New Barn. Rode Badger, Mabel Lorna Doone, Mother Brenda.

New covert blank; found Lodge Park; ran very nicely to Jolly's Gorse where we lost. Sherborne coverts on New Barn side of river blank. Found in Sherborne Cow Pastures, ran through Farmington Grove and Furzehill Wood and on as if for Gilbert's Grave; then right-handed and down through Clapton Gorse; a small circle in the vale and back on to the hill, where scent failed. Fox had been viewed back into Clapton Gorse but too far ahead. Good day.

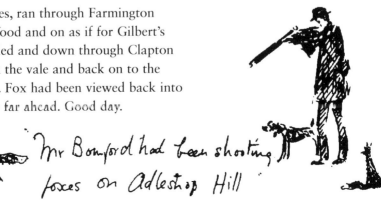

"Mr Bomford had been shooting foxes on Adlestrop Hill"

Monday, Feb. 14th

Chapel House. Rode Kruger, Mabel Lancer, Mother Velocity.

Found in Walk Gorse but soon lost. Found in small cover near Rollright, ran a very twisting line never getting far from Rollright and finally killed in Over Norton Park. Salford Osiers, Adlestrop Hill, the Neats blank. Found just below Hill; ran to ground by Chastleton village. Harcombs and Baywell blank. I had to leave early for Kruger to catch 4.45 train at Kingham. They found again on Daylesford Hill and killed near Cornwell. A very good job to kill two foxes as they have been unlucky lately. Not a bad hound day, but too few foxes. Bumford has been shooting on Adlestrop Hill. I stayed at Ranger's Lodge.

Wednesday, Feb. 16th

Burford. Rode Badger, Mabel Lorna Doone, Brenda lame.

Beat the bounds out towards Witney all the morning and did not find. Found Bradwell Grove but soon lost. Patcat gorse blank. Found in gorse cover nearby, but there seemed hardly a scrap of scent, so we came home. Very bad day.

Francie's heart with the Navy not on the Hunting Field

Friday, Feb. 18th

Moreton. Rode Kruger, Mabel Lancer.

Found in Crawthornes and took a line by Broadwell Manor, above Mrs Thursby's, checked by Maugersbury, then on and lost by Nether Swell Manor. Found at Banks Fee, ran round a bit and then hounds went home about 2.30 on account of awful rainstorm! Average day.

Saturday, Feb. 19th

Salperton. Cotswold. Rode Badger, Mabel Lorna Doone.

A fearful wind and a bad day.

Tuesday, Feb. 22nd

Naunton. N. Cotswold. Rode Kruger, Mabel Lancer.

A soaking wet day. Found in the Brake (thank goodness), ran out to Harford Bridge over almost entirely plough and a bad scent. Found Lark Wood, ran to the Park Wall and lost. Found close to Temple Guiting but did little. Bad day.

Wednesday, Feb. 23rd

Adlestrop. Rode Badger, Mabel Lorna Doone.

Found in Oddington Ashes ran by the Upper Ashes, Icomb Cow Pastures and on across the Bledington brook as if for Bould Wood, but turned sharp right-handed ran up by Icomb over the hill, across the line, below the Spotted Pig and back into Oddington Ashes.

THE DIARY ENDS ON 23rd FEBUARY
Because Jack & Francie are "pairing"
So are the wild animals. Jack & Francie got married the following September

Margaret Waddingham as a young girl, c.1850.

The Heythrop Hounds with Stow church on the skyline.

The ford at Upper Slaughter.

A view of Upper Slaughter.

Above: Rockliffe House.
Right: Guiting Grange, painted during the Second World War.

Captain Jack Kennard with two children and six grandchildren in front of Temple Guiting House. In addition to the family group, Diana Akers Douglas is to the far right of the photograh.

Eyford Knoll.

Grange Hill, painted pre-war.

Susan Boone, a self portrait, c.1943.

Happy Valley near Eyford.

A watercolour of Margaret Waddingham with Sophie, Mabel and Frances.

A watercolour of Guiting Grange c.1850.

All of the paintings in this colour section are painted by Susan Boone, with the exception of these two watercolours and the two initial images.

The four children of Frances and Jack Kennard; Bobby, Susan, Nancy and John.

Part of the field.

Arrival at the meet.

No hunting in this weather!

Riding to the meet.